# 2001

HOUSEHOLD HINTS
& DOLLAR STRETCHERS

By Michael Gore

Illustrations by Albert Goldson

CONDENSED FROM
"ENCYCLOPEDIA OF HOUSEHOLD HINTS
AND DOLLAR STRETCHERS"
PUBLISHED BY HANOVER HOUSE,
A DIVISION OF DOUBLEDAY & COMPANY, INC.
575 MADISON AVENUE, NEW YORK 22, N.Y.
PUBLISHED 1957. REGULAR EDITION, $3.95

# CONTENTS

3

# THIRTY-FIVE WAYS TO GET THE MOST
# FROM YOUR MEAT DOLLAR

*"Variety is the spice of life"* means don't get in a rut when buying meats. Variety in meal planning adds appetizing surprises to menus, extra value to your meat dollar. Save money by knowing the different, lower-cost cuts that will turn out equally well when prepared in a wide variety of ways. Because of the constant change in supply and demand, one cut may be the best buy one day, while a different one may be a "special" another day. A "special" usually means that a particular cut is more plentiful on the day offered. The lower price helps to keep meat moving while it is fresh. Remember, there are more than 200 meat cuts from which to choose.

### BROIL? ROAST? BRAISE? OR SIMMER?

*Broil or pan-broil:* Club, T-bone, porterhouse, sirloin, round steaks; ground beef patties, hamburgers; rump roast, if prime. "London" broil (don't pan-broil) flank steak on preheated broiler pan, as close to heat as possible (first having coated the meat on both sides with softened butter or margarine) only long enough to sear the meat. Cut in thin, diagonal slices.

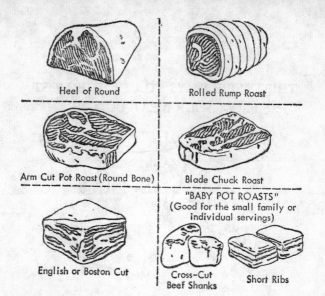

Heel of Round

Rolled Rump Roast

Arm Cut Pot Roast (Round Bone)

Blade Chuck Roast

English or Boston Cut

"BABY POT ROASTS"
(Good for the small family or
individual servings)

Cross-Cut
Beef Shanks

Short Ribs

*Roast:* Standing or rolled rib roast; rump roast, if prime meat.

*Braise:* Chuck roast, rump roast (both as pot roast), round steak, chuck steak, flank steak (this may also be scored, stuffed, and baked), short ribs, liver.

*Simmer:* Brisket (corned beef, if cured), plate, all stew meat (from chuck, shank, flank, neck, brisket, or heel of round), and all variety meats (heart, tongue, kidney, oxtail, sweetbreads). To prepare subsequently, braise all but tongue. Sweetbreads can be crumbed and baked or fried, or diced and creamed.

### WHERE THERE'S A VEAL THERE'S A WAY

*Broil or pan-broil:* Round steak, loin steak, loin chop, rib chop. Shoulder chops may be broiled, pan-broiled, or braised.

*Roast:* Round roast, rump roast, rib, breast (stuffed rolled shoulder).

*Simmer:* Stewing veal (shank, breast, neck), skillet steak (shoulder).

8

*Broil or pan-broil:* Leg steak, rib chop, loin chop, English lamb chop, Saratoga chop.

*Roast:* Leg (American or "Frenched"), loin end of leg, crown roast (rolled or straight), breast, boneless rolled shoulder.

*Braise:* Leg, shoulder, neck.

*Simmer:* Stewing lamb (neck, shank; both also for broth).

## ALL PORK MUST BE COOKED WELL

*When really fresh,* pork cuts are firm, fine-grained, grayish-pink in color, with a marble design of flecks of fat. On the outside, it is uniformly covered with firm white fat. Bones are pinkish, too, and porous inside when sawed. But when you prepare fresh pork cuts they must be cooked until thoroughly well done and no tinge of pink must remain.

*Broil, pan-broil, or fry:* Chops, ham, bacon, Canadian bacon, sausage, salt pork.

*Roast:* Loin roast, spareribs, fresh ham, whole tenderloin, fresh shoulder butt, fresh picnic shoulder, whole shoulder, whole or half ham, Canadian bacon (whole or piece), smoked butt.

*Braise:* Shoulder steak, rib chop, loin chop, tenderloin (whole or fillet), spareribs.

*Simmer:* Spareribs, boneless smoked butt, smoked picnic, ham shank, pigs' feet, hocks.

## TEN POINTERS ON MEAT STORING

1. *Fresh meat vs. fresh bacteria.* Remember meat is perishable. Even if you prepare it just several hours after you bring it home, put it in the refrigerator until you are ready to cook it. Unwrap the meat, wipe it, but don't wash it. Rewrap meat loosely in market or waxed paper. Another method is to place meat on a clear, dry plate or shallow dish and cover it loosely with waxed paper so air can circulate. If meat is not to be used the same day, put it in the coldest

**LAMB ROASTS**

Square-Cut Shoulder    Cushion-Style Shoulder    Boneless Rolled Shoulder

**VEAL ROASTS**

Shoulder Roast

Boneless Rolled Shoulder

**PORK ROASTS**

Loin, Rib End    Loin, Tenderloin End    Shoulder Butt (Boston Butt)

part of your refrigerator. Store prepackaged fresh meat the same way, first loosening original wrapper.

2. *Roasts and steaks.* The smaller the cut of meat, the sooner it should be used. Steaks and chops should be cooked within two or three days of purchase. Roasts may be stored slightly longer. Store broiling steaks in loose, clean wrapping paper. Keep frozen steaks frozen until you use them. They may be broiled without thawing, but allow longer time in the broiler.

3. *The "cold war" against spoilage* of small cuts. It's best to freeze small cuts if they are to be kept more than three days. If you don't have a home freezer, meat may be frozen in the frozen-food compartment or ice-cube section of your refrigerator. Use special freezer wrapping materials for long home-freezing storage. For short storage, a week or two, wrapping in heavy waxed paper and overwrapping with aluminum foil is adequate freezer wrapping. Wrap each chop or ground-meat patty separately with the paper. Packed closely, several may be overwrapped with one piece of foil. For refrigerator freezing, turn control to coldest position until meat is frozen.

4. *Variety meats are sensitive.* They spoil more quickly than other meats. Liver, kidney, sweetbreads, and cubed meat, especially, should be used within a day of purchase, and meanwhile kept under coldest refrigeration.

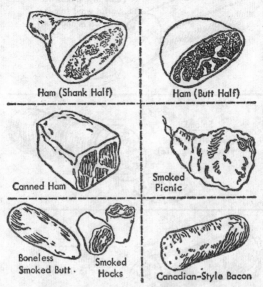

Ham (Shank Half)     Ham (Butt Half)

Canned Ham     Smoked Picnic

Boneless Smoked Butt ·    Smoked Hocks    Canadian-Style Bacon

5. *The smoked-meat department.* Smoked hams, bacon, sausage products like bologna, frankfurters, etc., require the same cold-storage care as fresh meat. Smoked hams and bacon should be used within a week. All prepackaged smoked meat may be stored in the original wrapper. Be sure package is well-sealed to prevent odors from spreading to the other foods in your refrigerator or freezer. By the same token, however, you can have smoked meat, lazy-Susan style, by wrapping fresh meat tightly with smoked meat. The fresh meat will acquire a smoky flavor.

6. *Cooked meat is perishable.* All cooked meats must be refrigerated. Store in a covered container or wrap tightly in waxed paper or aluminum foil.

7. *Are canned meats immune to spoilage?* Some are; some aren't. To make sure, check the can labels. The larger-size cans of luncheon meat and canned ham definitely need refrigeration. Smaller canned ham or picnic meat is usually

## SAUSAGE FOR COLD-CUT PLATTERS

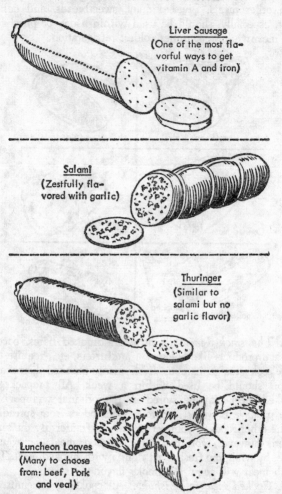

**Liver Sausage**
(One of the most flavorful ways to get vitamin A and iron)

**Salami**
(Zestfully flavored with garlic)

**Thuringer**
(Similar to salami but no garlic flavor)

**Luncheon Loaves**
(Many to choose from: beef, pork and veal)

well protected by the can itself, but to stay on the safe side read the labels.

8. *Keep frozen meat frozen.* Frozen meats packaged in moisture-proof wrapping may be stored for fairly long periods, but only in a home freezer and at 0°F., or lower. (It is

Liver, calves' - broil
or fry; beef - fry or
braise; pork - braise.

Heart - cook in
water or braise

Kidneys, lamb or
veal - broil or
fry; beef or pork
braise.

not advisable to home-freeze smoked and cured items like ham and bacon, because of their high salt content.) Once you thaw meat, use it. Never refreeze, except after it's been cooked in a form that lends itself to freezing leftovers.

9. *Venison* will retain its freshness from eight months to a year when frozen and provides an unusually interesting main dish any time of the year, not just in season.

10. *A dog's life* may be brightened, or that of any family pet, by freezing one-day-old portions of meats for pets, so any day can be a red-letter, red-meat day for them too.

*Note:* For general rules on freezing, see special freezer section, page 85.

### MIX IMAGINATION WITH LEFTOVERS

*Dressed-up leftovers* are fun to fix, fun to eat. They tax the imagination but not the budget.

13

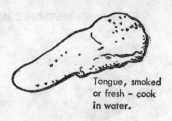

Tongue, smoked or fresh – cook in water.

Sweetbreads – precook in water 15 minutes, then braise, fry, broil or use in creamed dishes..

Brains – precook in water 15 minutes, then cream, scramble with eggs, or crumb and fry.

Tripe – cook in water until tender, then braise, fry or serve in tomato sauce.

*Three inexpensive lamb shanks* will serve six people if, after cooking until tender, the bone is removed and a whole cooked carrot put in the center of each shank. Fasten with toothpicks, dip in egg and crumbs, brush with melted butter or margarine, and bake in a 400°F. oven for ten minutes.

*Leftover roast ends up in hash.* But if a small amount of the hash is left over, use it hot as a filler for sandwiches made from well-browned French toast.

*New idea for roast-beef bits.* Everyone knows about sandwiches and combinations with vegetables in casserole, but here's a new trick: Add them to canned beef for a hearty, different, luncheon main dish.

*Miniature art.* Grind leftover beef roast with a small onion. Store in a small covered dish in your refrigerator for several days. Let the family forget all about it, then spring it on them as midget meat loaves.

*Meat-and-mushroom muffins.* A small amount of leftover cooked beef may be ground and added to any standard muffin mixture. Serve the meat muffins hot, topped with a quick sauce made from undiluted mushroom soup.

*Your stock goes up* with meat stock used as the liquid in gelatins for molded meat loaves and aspics.

*Don't pour flavor down the sink.* Bacon drippings used for frying and for searing meat give it a fine, delicate flavor. But be sure to use a little less salt when you cook with bacon fat.

*Additional ways with meat drippings.* Use it as shortening for bran muffins; to make white sauce, onion sauce, tomato sauce; in bread stuffing for veal, poultry, fish; as blend in some vegetables and soups; in bread crumbs or cereals to top vegetable or fish casseroles; to flavor macaroni, noodles, spaghetti; to grease muffin pans, to fry eggs, for flavor and economy; to brown croutons; to add to meat loaves. For shortening, strain through three thicknesses of cheesecloth.

# POULTRY AND FOWL

INCLUDING ECONOMY AND WASTE-PREVENTION
HINTS, COOKING AND "KEEP FRESH" METHODS,
FRESH AND FROZEN DO'S AND DON'TS

*Checking on chicken.* The chickens you buy are either dressed or ready-to-cook. "Dressed" means that they are priced and weighed—and paid for—while the head and feet are still on, the entrails still in. This means you pay for waste that is about 25 per cent of the total cost. "Ready-to-cook" chickens are priced after head, feet, and viscera have been discarded. Ready-to-cook poultry must always come tagged with brand and weight, to identify it as to quality. All registered brands are under standardized, bird-by-bird, process-by-process, inspection by veterinarians. But—be sure your retail meat man, too, refrigerates his ready-to-cook poultry, as this is extremely important to good health.

*Chickens should be plump and pleasing.* Whether you buy dressed or ready-to-cook chicken, go by these quality checks: Look at the drumstick. Don't buy if the chicken's thigh is thin and the bone heavy. Look at the neck. If it is well-fleshed, the rest of the bird will probably be the same.

Be careful if it has a long, scrawny neck, though. White, blue-tinged skin is not the mark of aristocracy in a chicken. The best-meat chickens have light-yellow skin.

*What size chicken should you buy?* Here is an approximate guide to use when marketing. Chart gives amount per serving, not per person. Served with rice, macaroni, etc., chicken portions may be smaller.

### HOW MUCH TO BUY PER SERVING

*If ready-to-cook*

| | |
|---|---|
| For broiling | ¼ to ½ bird |
| For frying | ⅔ to ¾ lb. |
| For roasting | ⅔ to ¾ lb. |
| For stewing | ⅔ to ¾ lb. |

*If dressed*

| | |
|---|---|
| For broiling | ¼ to ½ bird |
| For frying | ¾ to one lb. |
| For roasting | ¾ to one lb. |
| For stewing | ⅔ to ¾ lb. |

*Larger birds may mean economy.* These are called fowl, hens, or stewing chickens. Their meat is less tender than that of smaller birds, but they are delicious when slow-cooked in moisture, and used in stew, fricassee with dumplings, chicken pies, or chicken à la king.

*Better buy turkey.* Because in larger birds there is less bone in proportion to meat than in smaller birds, turkey is often a better buy than chicken.

*The "new look" in turkeys.* A few years ago a new style of turkey was developed, a new breed of broad-breasted bird that gives you more white meat, less bone waste with each turkey as compared with traditional turkeys. The Beltsville turkey is one of these new birds. It's a junior-size four- to nine-pound turkey that suits the needs of the small family of three to six people.

*Frozen poultry.* Several good brands appear on packages of frozen poultry, whole, or in parts. You may buy whole-chicken broilers, fryers, roasters, stewing chickens, assortments of chicken breasts, legs, thighs, wings, chicken livers, giblets, hearts, gizzards—all cleaned and ready to cook, after thawing. You can buy frozen young hen turkeys, young tom turkeys, junior turkeys, Long Island ducklings, whole frozen capons that weigh about four pounds or over. These unsexed male birds have a large proportion of white meat and are packaged and prepared and eaten as roasters.

*Thaw frozen poultry completely before cooking.* There are three ways to do this:

1. *Place poultry in its original wrapper* or box in the regular compartment of your refrigerator for about five to six hours for every pound of bird. (Overnight for a chicken, two to three days for a large turkey.)

2. *For quicker thawing,* place whole birds in cool running water until just pliable enough to handle. This requires one to three hours. Do not allow to stand in water after thawing.

3. *Packages of cut-up chicken or parts* should be opened and contents placed on a rack in a shallow pan or tray until pieces can be separated. An electric fan, directed toward the thawing chicken, speeds the process.

*To keep it from spoiling, keep poultry right.* Boxed, frozen chicken should be kept frozen in frozen-food compartment of your refrigerator until you plan to thaw and cook the chicken.

*Fry-'n'-freeze.* While most fried foods should not be frozen for later use, fried chicken may be, if properly wrapped in moisture-proof, vapor-proof paper. May be eaten thawed-out and cold at picnics, or from lunch boxes.

*Frozen fresh chicken* is practical if you raise chickens for home consumption or have access to supply from a nearby farm, or in a season when chicken happens to be plentiful and low-priced.

### LITTLE TIPS THAT PAY BIG BONUSES

*Use a cigarette lighter* to singe pinfeathers left on dressed poultry. Result is neat, safe, quick, and singeing that doesn't smudge the skin of the fowl.

*Baked apple?* No, but stuff chicken with cored apples to keep meat moist and to add piquancy to flavor.

*When buying turkey quarters or breasts* for small occasional roast, allow ¾ pound for each serving.

*Fancy-pants for Christmas turkeys.* Fringe two pieces of

white or pink tissue paper or aluminum foil and wrap unfringed part around end of bird's legs. Foil will remain in place. Fasten paper fringe with fine thread of matching color.

*On a silver platter.* If turkey is too large for your platter, wrap a tray with aluminum foil and use it for serving.

*Cover leftover refrigerated chicken.* Its delicate flavor is lost and absorbs other food flavors easily. Don't try to keep cooked poultry more than a few days. Use it up as soon as possible in interesting leftover dishes, or wrap and freeze it.

*Before freezing chicken,* remove pinfeathers and then wash and clean the bird thoroughly. Chicken may be packaged in freezer paper, aluminum foil, Saran wrap, and other moisture-proof, vapor-proof covering. Double-wrapping is recommended and be sure to date the package in order to avoid overlong freezer storage.

*Freeze chickens whole for roasting,* split for broiling, or cut up and packaged for frying. Pack the parts separately, if you wish, breasts in one package, thighs in another, etc. Giblets should always be packaged separately.

### DON'T FLIRT WITH FOOD POISONING

*Stuff bird just before roasting.* Don't stuff ahead of time, not even if you are going to refrigerate or freeze it.

*Scoop out leftover stuffing* from a roast chicken or turkey and refrigerate each separately, in covered dishes, or wrapped in waxed paper or aluminum foil. Stuffing should be used within two days. Fowl may be kept four to five days or longer if properly wrapped and frozen.

*Never stuff a chicken or turkey* with warm stuffing, then hold overnight before roasting.

*Never let gravy, dressing, or cooked poultry* stand at room temperature for even a few hours. Refrigerate them right after finishing the meal.

*Never partially roast a large turkey* one day, then leave it out of the refrigerator overnight to be completed the following day. If need be, get up early and put it in the oven before breakfast if you want to serve it at noon.

# CARVE LIKE A CONNOISSEUR

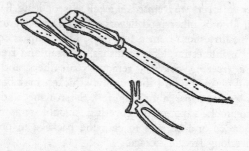

*Carving skillfully* takes a little practice, but it's neither tricky nor hard. And it's worth a little practicing, because when a perfectly cooked meat is properly carved, it is served at its appetizing best.

*A sharp knife* is the first requisite of good carving. (Don't use the carving knife for kitchen chores. When not in use, keep the carving set in its own box.) And do allow enough space on the platter for the carved slices, or give the carver an extra plate for them.

*Don't crowd the platter* with too much in the way of garnishes. The carver needs room to work.

*Meat is carved* across, not with, the grain. Slices should be uniform in thickness. Long, steady strokes of the knife produce smooth slices.

## STANDING RIB ROASTS

*Have backbone loosened by meat man* and then removed in kitchen after roasting. Use large carving knife. Set the roast on the platter, rib bones to the left, large end away from carver. Insert fork, guard up, between two top rib bones. Cut slices from outer fat edge to bones, making slices no thicker than ¼ inch.

*Free each slice* by running point of knife along edge

where it joins bone, and lift off before starting next slice.
When you have sliced below first bone, free it from roast
and lay to one side.

## T-BONE OR PORTERHOUSE

*Use small carving knife.* Place steak on platter with flank
(tail of steak) at carver's left. Cut around the T-bone to free
it from the meat. Lay bone to one side. Make cuts clear
across steak, making uniform wedge-shaped portions. Cut
flank into serving pieces. In serving, place on each plate a
piece of the larger or top muscle, a piece of tenderloin, and,
if desired, a piece of the flank.

## POT AND ROLLED ROASTS

*With point of knife,* cut around blade bone and remove
it. Trim off other bones. If roast is thin, slice across muscles.

For thicker roasts, turn section on its side and carve across the grain.

*For rolled rib roast* use large carving knife. Place roast on platter with the cut surface down. Insert fork, guard up, into the left side of the roast, an inch or two from the top. Make slices across the grain, starting at the far right side. Remove each cord only as you approach it. Cut the cord with the tip of the knife, loosen it with the fork, and lay to one side.

### WHOLE HAM

*Bring the ham to the table with the fat side up,* as this is the decorated portion—but turn the ham on its side for carving. The leg bone divides the ham into two unequal portions. The thick or chunky side of the ham will yield larger, more attractive slices called "horseshoe" slices. In order to carve these easily, first cut several lengthwise slices off the thinner side to form a base on which to rest the ham during carving.

*Now* cut a small wedge-shaped piece from the shank end (where the bone protrudes). This cut should be made just inside the knuckle. Then cut slices right down to bone.

*When a sufficient number of slices has been cut,* slip the knife in at the wedge and cut along the bone to free all of the horseshoe slices at once.

### PORK LOIN ROAST

*Have the backbone loosened.* When you take the roast out of the oven, remove the backbone before sending the roast to the table. Place the roast on the platter with the rib ends up, and rib side of the roast in front of the carver. Slice downward between the ribs, to make chop-sized servings. If the loin roast is a large one, it is possible to serve a boneless slice between each rib.

### FOWL

*Carver places platter so neck of bird is to his left,* and sticks fork astride breastbone. Leg and thigh bone are separated from nearest side by cutting at thigh joint, pressing leg away from body. With carving fork still in place, next separate nearest wing in same manner, cutting around wing joint to locate exact dividing point of joint, then sever wing completely. Now breast meat is ready to be sliced. Start at angle near tip of breastbone. Cut thin slices, always working toward joint where wing was removed. Then separate thigh from leg at joint; in the case of turkey, cut thin slices from these two pieces. For second helpings, turn platter, repeat same process on other side.

*Carving board for family dinners.* Nails driven through from underneath will hold roast securely in place for carving. Rubber feet on bottom surface will keep board from slipping around on the platter.

*Keep hubby happy when he's carving.* Be patient and tactful during operation. Add liberal helping of praise. If guests are present, keep conversation going cheerfully and never correct or direct the carving.

# FISH 'N-TIPS

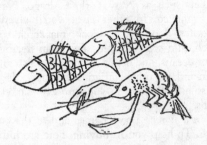

*Add variety and new taste treats to your menus* with fish and shellfish. You have more than 200 varieties to choose from since modern transportation and refrigeration methods make most of them available to you at your local markets or fish stores.

*Water animals used as food are divided into two groups:* Fish (vertebrates) and shellfish (invertebrates). Fish are covered with scales or, occasionally, with just a scaly-looking skin. Shellfish are covered with some type of shell.

*Shellfish have dual identities.* There are two types: Mollusks and crustaceans. Mollusks such as oysters and clams are very soft in structure and are protected by hard shells. The crustaceans, such as lobsters, crabs, shrimp, and crayfish, are covered by segmented, crustlike shells.

*Fish differs from meat.* Protein food though fish is, its water content is higher than that of meat and its extractives are lower. This means that the flavor of fish is more delicate. Meat cookery is more concerned with tenderness than with the development of flavor. Fish and some shellfish are already tender, so cooking must develop flavor.

*Varieties of fish differ,* as far as fat content is concerned. Most have lower fat content than medium beef. Exceptions are salmon, mackerel, butterfish, catfish, and turbot. All shellfish are low in fat content.

*Your success in cooking fish and shellfish* depends first upon your buying skill. Fish aren't only seasonal but also regional to some extent. Many varieties are shipped into the large markets such as New York, Chicago, New Orleans, and San Francisco. In other areas you'll always find the seven favorites—flounder, haddock, mackerel, cod, halibut, ocean perch, and whiting—plus fish from nearby lakes, rivers, bays, or oceans, and a variety of frozen fish and shellfish. As the demand for other varieties increases, they'll become available, so ask for them in your grocery market or at your fish dealer's.

*What's in a name?* Local names add to the confusion in buying fish. To help you in buying, here are individual fish descriptions and market forms:

*Whole or round fish.* Marketed just as it comes from the water. Fish sold this way must be scaled or skinned, eviscerated, and head, tail, and fins removed, if desired, before cooking.

*Drawn fish.* Marketed with the entrails removed. Fish must be scaled or skinned and head, tail, and fins removed, if desired, before cooking.

*Dressed fish.* Marketed scaled and eviscerated, usually with head, tail, and fins removed. These are ready to cook as purchased or, if large, can be split.

*Steaks.* These are slices, cut crosswise, of larger dressed fish. They vary from ½ to 1½ inches in thickness and are ready to cook as purchased. Chunks are pieces cut from large dressed fish. They vary in size and weight and are usually used for poaching or steaming. They are also usually cut to order.

*Fillets.* These are practically boneless pieces cut from the sides of fish. They are ready for cooking.

*Butterfly fillets.* They are two sides of a fish cut away from the backbone but held together by the flesh of the underside of the fish. They are ready for cooking.

*Cured fish.* Many salt- and fresh-water fish are cured by

smoking, drying, salting, or pickling in brine. Smoked and dried fish are generally split. Salted and pickled fish are available whole, split, or cut into small pieces.

*Cold smoked fish,* such as finnan haddie and kippered herring, are cured and partially dried at about 90°F., for a few hours. These will keep only a short time unless frozen. Cold smoked fish, such as boneless herring, that are processed for a longer time and are drier, will keep longer.

*Hot-smoked fish* are smoked at temperatures from 150°F., to 200°F., and are partially or wholly cooked. They will keep for only a short time unless frozen. Whitefish, lake herring, lake trout, buffalo fish, eels, and sturgeon are typical fish that are hot-smoked. The most popular is herring, called bloater and buckling in some areas.

*Dried fish* may be either air- or heat-dried. Thoroughly dried, salted or not, fish will keep indefinitely. But it must be rehydrated before using. Haddock, cod, hake, pollock, and cusk are fish that are usually dried.

*Salted fish* are either dry-salted or brine-cured. Brine-cured fish, such as herring are ready for eating after having been soaked in fresh water. Or they may be pickled.

*When buying fresh fish,* look for these signs of real freshness:

1. *Eyes* — bright, clear, full, transparent, and somewhat protruding. The eyes of stale fish often are cloudy or pink and somewhat sunken.
2. *Skin* — shiny and full-colored. Stale fish skin looks faded.
3. *Gills* — red and clean-looking. Gills of stale fish are gray, brownish, or greenish.
4. *Flesh* — firm and adhering to the bones.
5. *Odor* — fresh. "Fishy" odor associated with fish only develops as fish are held. It should not be disagreeably strong.

### FROZEN FISH HAVE QUALITY STANDARDS TOO

1. *Odor* — little or no odor. Poor quality frozen fish have strong fishy odor.
2. *Flesh* — solidly frozen with no discoloration or brown-

ing. Fish thawed and refrozen are usually poor in quality.

3. *Wrapping* — steaks and fillets should be wrapped in moisture-proof material with little or no air space between fish and wrapping.

4. *Glazing* — whole fish in the round or dressed are often frozen with a glaze of ice to prevent drying and freezer burn. This glaze should be intact.

*Seafood: Live, fresh, or frozen.* Alive, in-the-shell hard- and soft-shell crabs, lobsters, oysters, clams, and crayfish are marketed alive in the shell. Sometimes crabs and lobsters are sold cooked in the shell. Shells of live seafood should be tightly closed. Shellfish may also be bought as fresh or frozen shucked meat.

*Lobsters,* when bought alive, should show movement of the legs and the tail should curl under the body. When cooked in the shell, lobster should be bright red in color and without strong and disagreeable odor. Cooked meat should be white, sweet-smelling, and always held or displayed on ice.

*Shrimp* should have firm meat texture, mild odor. Shells are grayish-green, pinkish-tan, or pink, depending on variety. "Green" shrimp is a market term for shrimp that have not been cooked. Shrimp are usually priced according to size, the larger ones higher in price. Size, however, does not affect quality.

*Crabs* should be alive in the shell as hard-shell the year round, or alive in the shell as soft-shell in warm months only. In-the-shell crabs should show movement of the legs if bought alive. When cooked in the shell, they should be bright red in color and without disagreeable odor. Cooked meat should be milky white, sweet-smelling, and always held or displayed on ice.

*Scallops* are sold shucked fresh or frozen. Fresh scallops are white, larger and less expensive than bay scallops that are creamy, light tan, or pinkish in color. They should have a sweet, pleasant odor and be practically free of liquid.

*Mussels* should be alive in the shell, bought by the pound. (Very high food value.)

*Clams* should be alive in the shell. If the shell is open it should close tightly when tapped. Discard any clams that remain open. Shucked clams should be creamy in color, plump, with clear liquor, and free from pieces of shell.

*Lobster tails* (rock-lobster or spiny) are usually sold frozen. They are sections of ocean crayfish. The meat should be whitish, tightly closed.

*Oysters.* Gaping shells that do not close when tapped indicate dead oysters that should be discarded. Shucked oysters should be creamy in color, plump, with clear liquor, and free from pieces of shell. The liquor should not exceed ten per cent by weight of the total.

*Crabmeat and lobstermeat* are sold fresh-cooked in pry-open cans, useful in quick main dishes, as well as in salads.

P.S., P.S., AND P.S.

*Rare tidbit on rarebit.* Leftover or canned seafood makes a welcome rarebit difference. Add tomato juice instead of milk, and see for yourself.

*A live minnow is a good minnow.* Minnows will stay alive much longer, when transported, if you add six or eight drops of iodine to the water.

*Don't let smell tell a fishy story.* To keep your hands from smelling fishy, when you prepare fish, chill fish thoroughly in cold water before you touch it.

*The fish that didn't get away.* Those fish needn't be so slippery when you handle them if you first dip your fingers in salt.

# STRETCHING THE EGG & DAIRY DOLLAR

*To keep milk fresh to the last drop,* cover and refrigerate as soon as received. Wipe the container with a clean, damp cloth and never touch or wipe the pouring lip when it has been kept sterile by a covering cap.

*Milk in the freezer.* Pasteurized, homogenized milk may be frozen for periods up to 2 weeks in original container. Caution: pour off a little before freezing, because you need a 2-inch air space at the top of the container to allow room for expansion during freezing.

*Fresh milk stays fresh longer* if you add a pinch of salt to a quart of fresh milk.

*Before boiling milk,* rinse the pan in cold water. Keeps milk from sticking to the pan.

*Milk may be scalded* in a double boiler. That way you don't have to worry about boiling over or scorching.

*After opening can of evaporated milk,* plug the openings with neat little rolls of waxed paper. Keep can holes from being sealed over with dried milk, lets milk pour freely when plugs are removed.

*Cream whips faster.* Add 6 or 8 drops of lemon juice per pint (2 cups) of cream. Use an eye dropper and count them; too much lemon sours the cream.

*Cream won't curdle* when poured over berries or fruits if you mix a small pinch of baking soda with the cream before serving.

*Easy-to-spread consistency* is best achieved by setting on a small plate or butter dish the amount of butter you will require and leaving this at room temperature for about 10 minutes. Melting or quick melting of large quantities spoils freshness of the butter you don't use right away.

*Cream butter* in a hurry with your electric mixer. First cut up into pieces with a clean knife, to give the mixer a good start.

*Store perishable soft cheese,* as you do milk, in the refrigerator in a tightly covered container. Buy in amounts to be used in a short time. Other cheeses keep well in a cold place if wrapped so that air is kept out. Foil is fine for this.

*Refrigerate packaged cheese* in its original container, using additional waxed paper or aluminum foil, if necessary, to rewrap the cheese. Wrap unpackaged cheese tightly with waxed paper, laminated foil or vinegar-dampened cloth before refrigerating. An overwrap that's convenient for paper or cloth is a non-porous pliofilm bag such as you use in freezer storage.

*If mold forms on cheese,* it may be scraped away with no harm to the cheese. Should cheese become dry, grate it and keep in covered container. It's good for cooking.

*Cheese (except cottage)* tastes best when served unchilled. Take it from the refrigerator long enough before serving to reach room temperature.

*Cheese grates easily* if it has been chilled first. So grate it the moment you take it from the refrigerator.

*To prevent curdling, scorching, and stringiness* in foods made with cheese or milk, cook at low, low temperatures and don't overcook.

*Cheese and fruit.* They were "meant for each other."

Serve Roquefort cheese with fresh pear sections; Tokay grapes with Liederkranz cheese; orange sections with Swiss and cream cheese; apples with Camembert; pieces of apple, cheese, and pears, speared on toothpicks.

*Cream-cheese spread.* Soften a 3-ounce package of cream cheese with 1 tablespoon each of tomato catsup and fresh lemon juice. Add a bit of finely chopped parsley for garnish.

## THE EGG AND YOU

*Tips on egg storage.* Always keep in refrigerator. Unbroken eggs should be in covered containers; otherwise they lose moisture and absorb odors, because shells are porous. Yolks keep best if covered with water; whites should be kept in tightly covered jar.

*If you keep all your eggs in one basket,* pencil-mark left-over eggs, so that you'll use them up first.

*To test the age of an egg,* place in deep pan of cold water. If it lies on its side, it is fresh. If it stands at an angle, it is probably 3 or 4 days old. If the egg stands on end upright, it is over 10 days old. If it floats to the top, toss it out!

*To keep eggs fresh* for a fairly long time, rub very fresh eggs with oil, butter, or pure glycerin over the entire surface of the shell.

*Don't freeze* cooked foods containing hard-cooked egg whites. Egg white changes in texture rapidly, toughens, and tends to develop off flavors when frozen.

*Egg-peeling tip.* By adding salt to the water in which eggs are hard-cooked, you harden the shell and make it much easier to peel off.

*To separate egg whites and yolks,* the for-sure no-broken-yolk way, puncture a small hole at one end of the shell. This releases the white into a collecting bowl and yolk stays inside. Break shell, remove yolk whole.

*Simmer eggs.* Boiling water is not recommended, since both yolks and whites coagulate at temperatures below the boiling point of water. Simmer soft-cooked eggs 3 minutes for very soft, 4 minutes for firm whites but soft yolks, 5 minutes for folks who like 'em a little longer but still on the soft side. Eggs simmer to hard-cooked stage in 10 minutes, but without any of the usual green division between white and yolks that develops when eggs are boiled. No hard-boiled-egg odor either.

*Is that stray egg hard-cooked or raw?* To test, place the egg on its side and spin it like a top. If the egg spins on an even keel, it is cooked. If it wobbles, it's raw.

*When beating egg whites,* be sure to use an enamel, stainless-steel, glass, or porcelain bowl. Never use aluminum, because eggs darken aluminum-ware.

*Egg whites beat up quicker and higher* if you add a tiny pinch of salt and let them stand until they're room temperature before you beat them.

*Eggs-pansion.* You get expanded volume from beaten eggs, when they are at room temperature rather than just out of the refrigerator. So, let them warm up by removing them from the cold ½ hour to 1 hour in advance.

# FIFTY-FOUR WAYS TO BE CLEVER
# WITH VEGETABLES

FOR WASTELESS BUYING, STORING, PREPARATION,
LEFTOVER USE

*The storing story.* Generally, fresh green vegetables are most safely stored in the refrigerator if not used the same day you bring them home. Still, there are a few little tricks to know:

*Certain vegetables keep better if stored "as-is."* Store peas and lima beans in the pod, corn in the husk (to preserve full food value and prevent shriveling).

*Keep corn on the cob fresh.* When you have to keep it a day or longer before serving, slice a small piece off the stalk end and stand ears in a pan containing an inch of water. Let outside leaves stay on.

*Goes to their heads.* The tops of carrots, beets, turnips, and parsnips should be cut off before the vegetables are stored. Tops draw the moisture and food value from the roots, leaving them wilted and limp.

*Keep parsley fresh.* Place in fruit jar, close lid tight, and keep in the refrigerator.

*Refrigerator can revive bargain vegetables.* Many food dealers will sell slightly wilted leafy vegetables at reduced prices. Before storing, wash them; place in crisper drawer while still moist. Process often restores crispness completely.

*To freeze or not to freeze,* that is the question. Each vegetable reacts in a different way. It's worth knowing.

*Let the Government help you.* Some varieties of vegetables and fruits are better adapted to freezing than others. When planting a garden or buying vegetables for freezing, consult Agricultural Extension Service Department at your state university to learn about varieties grown in your locality that are considered best for freezing.

*Do not freeze* lettuce, celery, raw tomatoes, or carrots. They lose crispness when frozen.

*Quality counts.* In choosing fruits and vegetables for freezing, buy the best. Properly packaged, you get out of the freezer exactly what you put into it. Freezing does not improve low-grade foods.

*Get 'em while they're young.* With few exceptions (like winter squash and eggplant), buy "young" vegetables, before their starch content has developed. Prepare for freezing immediately after harvest or purchase. If this is impossible, store in refrigerator, but for not more than eight hours.

*Cooking frozen vegetables.* For best results, do not thaw (except corn on the cob or spinach) before cooking. Cook in very little water for as short a time as possible so vegetables are tender but still slightly crunchy.

*To thaw frozen vegetables.* Simply put them, package and all, in cold water.

*For faster cooking* of quick-frozen spinach and chopped broccoli, cut block into six or eight pieces. There are knives especially designed to do the job for you, though any good, sturdy, sharp knife will do.

*Asparagus and broccoli* will cook more quickly if you let frozen blocks thaw just enough so stalks separate, before you put them in water.

### LITTLE-KNOWN TRICKS WITH WELL-KNOWN VEGETABLES

*Laundering spinach.* You'll save many washings if you soak spinach first in salt water.

*Wash leafy vegetables,* such as spinach, just before cooking. Add no water; enough clings to the leaves, from washing water, to cook them.

*Clean newly dug garden vegetables easily.* Place in wire egg-gathering basket and spray with garden hose. Basket holds generous supply of vegetables.

*How to "chop" parsley.* Away with the tedious old wooden bowl and chopping tool. Separate tufts from stems. Either cut the parsley with one of the new patented cutters or gather it firmly in the left hand, cutting through it with a knife or scissors.

*Know your onions and shed no tears.* Next time you slice onions, spear a one-inch chunk of bread on the point of your paring knife before peeling. Bread absorbs those tear-jerking fumes.

*Un-grate-ful carrots?* You'll grate carrots without sustaining wounds if you leave at least an inch of the green tops on. Use them as handles and you can grate the vegetable with ease.

*To extract juice from an onion.* Cut a slice and scrape the onion over the finest part of your grater. Or simply scrape a sharp knife across the cut edge, working over a small bowl. You'll soon have that teaspoonful of juice many recipes call for.

*Skip the bowl,* if you have a sense of adventure, and scrape the onion juice right into the mixture that calls for it. A few drops more or less don't matter and you save washing one dish.

*Beets peel easily* if they are dipped in cold water immediately after they are boiled. Don't soak 'em, though. They bleed easily. And remember to leave an inch of stem on beets when you cook them. Cut too close, they really bleed.

*Whiter cauliflower.* Cauliflower will come to the table much whiter if a piece of lemon is added during cooking. Overcooking tends to darken cauliflower, so cook only until tender.

*Candid advice on candied vegetables.* You love 'em. But you hate washing the pan afterward. Who doesn't? Even a dishwasher rebels. Heat the greased pan before adding the sugary mixture. Doesn't it wash a whole lot easier?

*An asparagus tip.* Always open cans of whole asparagus spears from the bottom so that the tips won't break as you ease the spears out of the can.

*Don't buy squishy squash.* Save money on squash. Select only squash that is heavy for its size, with clear complexion and firm, smooth rinds. Blemishes and scars and soft rinds may mean you're wasting your money.

*For crisp celery*, immerse in ice-cold water, with a couple of ice cubes added for good measure, for a few moments before serving.

*Pliers ply their trade*, when you open a jar of home-canned vegetables or fruit. Use the pliers to grip the rubber ring, and screw cap or glass lid loosens in a jiffy.

*Identify with glamour.* Save those good-enough-to-eat pictures of fruits and vegetables from the magazines, then paste them on the appropriate jars when you do your canning. Makes each one look more appetizing and "pretty as a picture."

*Corn off the cob.* The kernels of sweet corn are a cinch to remove if you use a shoehorn. The wide end of the horn is just right for shearing the kernels off.

CALLING A SPUD A—POTATO

*Spuds are temperamental.* Cooked potatoes do not freeze well in liquid. They become mushy and grainy, so leave them out of frozen stews, meat pies, or casseroles. Mashed and stuffed potatoes, however, can be frozen. For mashed potatoes, cook as usual but mash through potato ricer so there will be as little air in mixture as possible.

*Add a little milk* to the water in which you boil potatoes. Improves tastiness immensely, prevents them from turning black. Another way to keep potatoes white is to add a teaspoon of vinegar to the cooking water.

*Baked potatoes in half the time.* Parboil them for about five minutes before draining and drying potatoes and putting them into the oven and they'll bake in about half the usual time.

*Note to K.P.'s.* Don't throw away half of that highly nutritious potato by peeling it. Rub the skin off, instead, with one of those new metal pot cleaners. These are just rough enough to rub off the outer skin without wasting the body of the potato.

*Fingers stained?* Remove vegetable stains from your fingers by rubbing them with a slice of wet potato.


### A WAY—NOT AWAY—WITH LEFTOVERS

*Peas pep up leftovers.* If vegetables like string beans, broccoli, corn, carrots, or beets are among your leftovers, use them with canned peas in a mixed-vegetable salad, served with French or Russian dressing.

*Don't throw away beet tops.* They're delicious cooked and are rich in vitamins and minerals, especially iron.

*Add a few empty pea pods* to peas and to soup when cooking; they add flavor. But fish them out before serving either; they're too tough to eat except when they are garden-fresh and cooked with tender young peas, when you eat pod and all.

*A little leftover spinach,* finely chopped, adds intrigue and color to the batter for luncheon waffles. Or, mixed with chopped hard-cooked eggs in a white sauce, it becomes part of a topping for waffles.

*Save leftover broccoli* to decorate next day's casserole of whipped potatoes. Push stems into potatoes, with just the blossoms showing. Brush with melted butter or margarine and put in oven, at 350°F., to brown, for about 15 minutes.


### YOUR SALAD DAYS ARE NEVER OVER

*Can you take two dozen?* Chances are no salad, however "mixed," is likely to contain all 24 basic greens that make up the salad family. But, there they are, and one way or another, they are all being used in healthful, wonderful green salads.

*Roll call.* Here are their names: Four kinds of lettuce (iceberg, Boston, leaf, bibb); four kinds of cabbage (savoy,

Chinese, green, red); escarole, romaine, chicory, French endive, water cress, mustard greens, dandelion greens, beet greens, field salad, nasturtium leaves, spinach, kale, celery tops, sour grass, turnip greens, finochio.

You'll serve more salads if you store greens washed and ready to use, wrapped in aluminum foil or in your refrigerator hydrator. Ready enough greens to last a week to ten days by draining them and sealing them into envelopes in foil. They'll remain crisp and garden-fresh for as long as they last and will always be ready for tossing into delicious salad mixes.

### ALL THE SALAD TRIMMINGS

Salads are exciting with nongreen extras mixed in or parading on top.

Here are a few colorful ideas:

For trim orange or grapefruit sections, set fruit on board; then, with a sharp knife, whittle off peel in strips, cutting from top to bottom, and deep enough to remove all white membrane. Next cut along both sides of such dividing membrane, and lift out each section. Work over a bowl at this point, so you catch all the juice.

Tomatoes are first choice. Add them at the last minute, so they won't thin dressing. Also, cut them in vertical slices, the way the French do. Keeps more juice in.

Radish roses are most decorative, but thin slices or coarse shreddings perk up salads too.

Celery stalks lend themselves to a variety of strips, depending on whether you cut them thin, diagonal, or lengthwise; or fringe both ends, soak them in ice water, and turn them into celery curls.

Carrots curl around your finger if the shaving is thin. Use a vegetable parer for this shaving. They chill, in ice water, and stay curled better than a permanent wave.

Mushroom disks are a delicacy. Use fresh, raw, whole, unpeeled, washed, young mushrooms, and slice either lengthwise or crosswise. Drained canned whole or sliced mushrooms are fine too, for salads.

Raw cauliflower (or broccoli) yields beautiful, delicious tiny flowerets. Or slice bigger flowerets into wafer-thin fans.

41

*Cucumber slices* for cool summer salads are a natural. Or, to make it more festive still, make cucumber curls by slicing unpeeled cucumbers lengthwise, very thin with a vegetable parer. Spread with cream-cheese spread and roll up jelly-roll fashion. Fasten ends with colored toothpicks. Chill until ready to serve.

*Cream-cheese spread.* Soften a three-ounce package of cream cheese with one tablespoon each of tomato catsup and fresh lemon spread. Add a bit of finely chopped parsley for garnish.

# LITTLE KNOWN TIPS ABOUT
# FRUITS AND BERRIES

—YOU'RE BOUND TO SAVE MONEY, WORK, AND . . .

## WHAT YOU SHOULD KNOW ABOUT FRUITS AND BERRIES

*To cut up fresh pineapple,* cut washed pineapple into ½-inch crosswise slices. Remove core from each slice with a pointed sharp knife or the "hole" part of a doughnut cutter. Next, peel outer edge of slices, cutting deep enough so you remove the eyes. You can serve the pineapple sliced or cut the slices into thin wedges.

*Pineapple used in gelatin desserts* should be either canned or cooked. Raw pineapple, and fresh-frozen, contain an enzyme that prevents proper jelling.

*Crushed pineapple.* A clever way to crush pineapple is to run it through your meat chopper. Looks wonderful. Be sure, of course, to trap the juice. And with a little liquid added, you can crush pineapple in seconds in an electric blender.

*To make melon balls,* or apple, cantaloupe, avocado, canned jellied cranberry sauce balls, use French ball cutter. If you haven't one, the teaspoon of your measuring set (or the ½-teaspoon size if you like smaller balls) is an excellent tool too.

*Frozen fruit looks best,* tastes best if served when just thawed, while there are still a few ice crystals left.

*When thawing time is short,* put unopened carton of quick-frozen fruit in a bowl of water and let it stand about 25 minutes. Fruit will be thawed and ready to serve when you open the container.

*Fresh berries.* Spread berries out on tray and store in refrigerator on an open sheet. Chill, but do not wash until shortly before serving. Then place in colander, and run cold water gently over berries. If there are hulls, remove after washing, to save flavor.

*Keep strawberries firm,* even if you must store them several days before using. Put them in the refrigerator in a colander. The cold air, circulating through the berries, will keep them firm and fresh.

*Cold, but not too cold.* To enjoy its full flavor, remove fruit from refrigerator a little ahead of serving, so that it can warm up a bit. (Remember not to store bananas in the refrigerator.)

*Prevent darkening of fruits.* For those fruits that have a tendency to darken in freezing, add ¼ teaspoon ascorbic acid (vitamin C) to each cup of syrup. You can buy the ascorbic acid at the drugstore.

*For economy's sake,* read lables on canned fruits. Often the same food packed in heavy syrup is more costly (and higher in calories for weight watchers) than that packed in lighter syrup. By checking weights listed, you can choose the product that gives most for your money.

*"Look, Mom, no hands."* To slice banana without touching it with your fingers, peel it down all around except for one segment. Hold thumb against that strip of peel and cut against it.

*Save time when peeling pears or peaches.* First scald fruit with boiling water, then peel. Skins come off much easier that way.

*For good-looking baked apples,* prick their skins beforehand. They'll bake without bursting. Extra-flavor tip: A dried apricot or a few raisins in the core with the sugar and spices.

*Apple to the rescue.* A slice of apple added to each pint of cranberries before cooking will greatly improve the flavor without sacrificing any of the tartness.

*Place a cut apple* in your cookie jar or fruit-cake box. It will keep soft cookies soft and fruit cake moist. Caution: Don't store apples with crisp cookies.

### NUTS ARE FRUITS TOO

*Botanically, nuts are fruits.* They're fruits from trees and contain a kernel enclosed in a shell. All we care about is the kernel, of course, since shells are not edible. (Peanuts aren't nuts or fruits; they're legumes!)

*Nuts we use the most* include almonds, Brazil nuts, butternuts, cashew nuts, chestnuts, filberts or hazelnuts, hickory nuts, pine nuts, pistachios, and the different varieties of English, black, and other walnuts.

*Hotel chef's trick.* Ever wonder how hotel chefs make those delicious long slivers of Brazil nuts for their salads and desserts? Here's their secret: Cover shelled Brazil nuts with cold water, bring slowly to a boil, simmer two or three minutes, then cool. Skins come off easily afterward and you'll find them in expensive restaurants.

*Blanching almonds.* Pour boiling water over shelled almonds, permitting them to stand until the brown skin has loosened. Pinch off skin after nuts have cooled. To whiten blanched almonds, soak in cold water in your refrigerator.

*To keep lemons for months,* after you buy them at a bargain, put the whole lemons into sterilized canning jars, cover with cold water, adjust rubber rings, and screw covers down tightly. Not only will they stay fresh for months, they'll yield much more juice than when you first bought them.

*Get more juice.* Even when you do no long-term storing, you get more juice from lemons, limes, and oranges if you soak them in a pan of water for a while before squeezing. Then, before cutting, roll the fruit around on the table with your hand.

*Strain without strain.* Moisten cheesecloth in water and wrap around end of lemon. Juice will strain-as-you-squeeze.

*Salt enhances sweet flavors.* Proper function of salt is to develop and bring out natural food flavors, not to make foods taste salty. Sprinkle small amount in fruit juices; it increases sourness of acids and increases sweetness of sugars.

*To peel an orange without spattering,* dig heel of paring knife into skin and draw it backward around middle of orange. Then insert smooth teaspoon handle into the cut, push down and around until you pry the skin loose. Remove one half at a time.

*When grating rind of lemon or orange,* be sure not to grate too deep. The colored part of rind gives the flavor while the white part causes food to taste bitter.

# AMAZING THINGS YOU CAN DO WITH
BREADS, ROLLS AND BISCUITS

*Tips that keep bread fresh.* If you store bread in a room-temperature place, such as your breadbox, it will stay soft but may not keep too long, especially in warm weather. If you store it in your refrigerator it will be safe from mold but will not remain soft. Compromise is to store bread in the refrigerator but wrap it first in waxed paper or other moisture-proof paper and then put it into a pliofilm bag. Double-wrapping keeps moisture in, refrigerator temperature keeps mold out.

*If you use lots of bread,* store it in your breadbox. But be sure to keep the box clean and free from old pieces of bread. Scald and/or sun the breadbox weekly.

*If you use little bread,* but have a freezing compartment in your refrigerator, double-wrap the bread as directed for refrigerator storage and store bread in the frozen-food compartment. You can keep several kinds of bread frozen simultaneously, have a choice of breads, and use only as much as you need at one meal.

*Can you freeze bakery bargains?* Baked foods (including yeast rolls, yeast bread, quick breads, cookies, unfrosted cakes and some frosted ones, and cup cakes) can be frozen for from two to three months. Buy them when your baker features specials, eat them when you want them.

*To prevent bread crust from cracking*, shelter fresh-baked bread from cold gusts of air or sudden drafts and winds on the heated surface.

*It does matter how you slice it.* It's easy to slice fresh bread as smoothly as if it were done by a slicing machine. Just heat the blade of the bread knife (but don't let the man of the house catch you at it—it's supposed to ruin the "temper" of the steel, according to all male experts) by passing it through a flame or placing it on a hot electric unit for a few moments.

*To keep peace in the family*, you'll find that a serrated bread knife does an excellent job without heating, moreover, saves you one step—the heating—when you slice bread.

*To freshen French bread, Italian bread, hard rolls*, cover crusts with cold water, using a pastry brush. Then place in 350°F. oven until crisp again, about ten minutes. Cool before slicing.

*Hard butter spreads easily* if you cream it first. To cream, beat butter vigorously with a wooden spoon. You can also use your electric mixer to do a quick job of creaming butter.

*Spreading trick for peanut butter.* Add a teaspoon of hot water just before spreading. Also makes the peanut butter go further.

*Let no crumbs scatter* when grinding dried bread. Catch them in a paper bag. Fasten opening of bag firmly around grinder outlet with tightly tied cord or a rubber band.

*Salt carton into bread-crumb box.* Empty salt cartons with spouts make excellent containers for bread crumbs ground from dried bread. Use funnel to get crumbs into carton.

## BISCUIT AND ROLL WIZARDRY

*Biscuits bake best* on baking sheet without sides. To insure proper heat circulation, sheets should be small enough to leave one or two inches of space between edges of sheet and sides and back of oven.

*No more pale-face biscuits.* Wan-looking baking-powder biscuits turn a healthy golden brown if you simply add a teaspoon of sugar to the recipe, with dry ingredients.

*Start with a biscuit mix* and use your imagination. Make a quick and succulent breakfast hot bread this way: Roll a recipe of biscuit mix into rectangular shape, about ¼ inch thick. Spread with melted butter or margarine. Sprinkle with brown sugar, raisins, and chopped nuts. Roll as you would a jelly roll. Cut into ½-inch slices. Bake on greased cookie sheet, cut side up, at 425°F., 15 to 18 minutes.

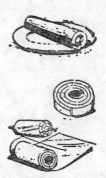

*The biscuit mix need not make biscuits.* Waffles, pancakes, dumplings, nut bread, fudge cake, chocolate-chip cookies, and breakfast crumb cake are only a few of the goodies you can make with biscuit mix. Simply follow package directions at first, then let yourself go on other uses of biscuit mix.

*To heat ready-to-eat bread and rolls,* wrap bread slices or rolls snugly in aluminum foil. Bake at 350°F., about 15 minutes, or until hot. If served in the foil wrapping, turn foil edges down to form a basket; they'll keep hot to the last crumb.

*Add your own trimmings to hot-roll mixes.* Make hot-cross buns from hot-roll mix by adding raisins to the dough as well as chopped citron, granulated sugar, cinnamon. Let rise until double in bulk. Shape ball-like buns. Place in greased cake pan. Let rise in warm place 30 to 60 minutes. With scissors, cut small cross in each bun. Bake at 400°F., 15 to 20 minutes. Combine confectioners' sugar with a little warm milk and vanilla extract to dip over hot bun and fill crosses.

# PRIZE-WINNING PIES

*Crust is the crux of the pie matter.* For flaky, tender-crust pastry that nevertheless has body, use all-purpose flour, sometimes called "family flour." Sift it just before making level measurements. You need the right kind of shortening too. Where a recipe specifies the kind of shortening or oil to be used, follow directions for best results.

*Liquid assets.* Liquid is the cement between flour and fat. The amount is, therefore, most important for consistency. Follow recipe specifications carefully. If there's too little liquid, dough falls to pieces. If there's too much, the pastry will be tough. Where the recipe says "about," start with less liquid, then add the rest gradually and cautiously.

*Roll right.* Unless recipe says otherwise, use a stockinet-covered rolling pin and flour lightly. Use a cloth-covered board. Roll the floured pin over the board twice, to rub the flour off on it lightly. Shape half of the dough into a ball on cloth. Flatten with patting motion of pin. Now make a circle by rolling lightly from the center of the dough in all directions. As you approach the edges, lift the rolling pin, to avoid splitting the edge of the dough or thinning it down too much. Occasionally lift dough to give it a quarter turn, but do not turn it over. If it seems to stick, lift it gently by slipping rubber spatula under edge and sprinkling a little flour on the cloth on the board. Not much, though, as too much flour toughens pastry. Continue to roll out until the circle is 12 inches in diameter. Make sure there are no cracks or holes into which the filling can later seep.

*Slitting pretty*. You can make these slits whether you do it over the filling or by first folding the upper crust in half. If you use the folding method, you can make the cuts through both halves of the circle, like cutting a paper doll.

Cut in pattern shown by dotted lines. This way the slits will form an exactly symmetrical design. If you make the slits after the top crust is in place over the filling, you can still follow the designs. Just disregard the fact that half of each design consists of dotted lines.

Let off steam from your pie another attractive way: Place top crust on filling, secure it at edge of lower crust. Then, with a small cutter in the shape of a heart, star, or bunny, make six cutouts evenly spread in a circle all through the top crust but do not remove the cutouts. (*See next page.*)

*Here are some pretty, yet easy, edgings* you can give your pie masterpieces. Caution: Where you use fork or skewer, dip them in flour before using.

*The last word IN crusts: Nut crust.* Make mixture of a cup of finely ground almonds, walnuts, pecans, or Brazil nuts and 2 tablespoons of granulated sugar. Use the back of a tablespoon to press mixture into pie plate, bottom and sides only, not the rim. Bake at 400°F. for eight minutes.

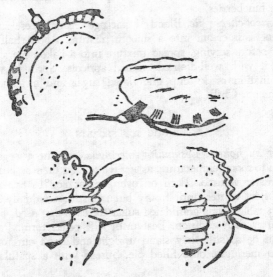

*The last word ON crusts: No-bake graham crust.* Make crumbs of graham crackers, then mix 1⅓ cups graham-cracker crumbs, ⅓ cup brown sugar, ½ teaspoon cinnamon, ⅓ cup melted butter. Reserve 3 tablespoons. With back of a tablespoon, press mixture into 9-inch, well-greased pie plate, bottom and sides only, not the rim. Chill very well, fill, then cover with the 3 tablespoons of the graham-cracker crumb mixture.

## PIE IDEAS THAT ARE DIFFERENT

*Mock pumpkin pie.* Few can tell the difference, yet this "pumpkin" pie is made from sweet potatoes or steamed squash. For an egg, substitute a tablespoon of cooked oatmeal beaten into the custard mixture.

*1-2-3 pie.* Step 1: Bake (or have ready) a 9-inch pie shell. Step 2: Fill shell with 3 cups sliced strawberries or peaches. Step 3: Top with whipped cream, sweetened or not. And there you are!

*Blueberry pie short cut.* Line a 9-inch pie plate with vanilla wafers or lemon snaps. Make an instant vanilla pudding from a package. Pour it into the wafer-lined pie plate. Chill. Just before serving, cover top with washed-and-dried fresh blueberries.

*Apricot-cheese pie.* Blend ¾ package cream cheese and a cup of sour cream into a smooth mixture. About half an hour before serving, spread mixture into a baked pie shell. Top it with well-drained canned apricots. Sprinkle with combination of ⅓ cup granulated sugar and a teaspoon cinnamon. Chill.

## MERINGUE TOP SECRETS

*For an honest, upstanding meringue,* set out 3 eggs to warm to room temperature, as egg whites can then be beaten to greater volume. Turn on oven, set at 400°F. Separate eggs. Beat whites until frothy but not stiff. Gradually add 2 or 3 tablespoons granulated sugar for each egg used, beating after each addition. Beat until stiff peaks form. Peaks should be so stiff they stand upright and don't curl over. Spoon meringue onto filled pie. Spread with a spatula so

that meringue touches inner edge of crust all around. This avoids shrinkage when baked. Pull up points all over the meringue with your spatula. Bake at 400°F. 8 to 10 minutes, until it turns a very delicate brown. It's done if it's dry to the touch. Cool on a rack and keep out of drafts.

*"Meringue lemon" pie.* That's not a printing error, but a different kind of pie. It's made with a meringue shell that brims out to a luscious, crinkly-looking picture-frame border. The baked meringue shell is filled with a velvety lemon cream. The edge of the shell is sprinkled with toasted shredded coconut. The delicious concoction then goes into the

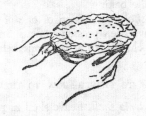

refrigerator for at least 12 hours, preferably overnight. For a real effect, decorate top with fresh strawberries in center and blobs of sweetened, freshly whipped cream "petals" with toasted shredded coconut "dew" on them.

*Fractureproof meringue cutting.* To keep your fragile, precious meringue topping from breaking up, come cutting time, sprinkle a little granulated sugar over it before cutting.

### FINE POINTS IN PIE BAKING

*Overjuicy pies need not run over.* Before baking, insert 1½-inch pieces of uncooked macaroni in several of the slits in the top crust. Remove macaroni before serving, of course. Or wrap wet pie tape around the rim before putting the pie in the oven. Or cut the vent slits nearer the center of the top

and away from the edges. Or make fluted or forked edge to help seal in the fruit juices.

*To make fruit pies less juicy,* try this: When preparing the filling, beat 1 egg white stiff, mix with the amount of sugar required for the filling, add 1 tablespoonful of flour, then mix thoroughly with fruit and other ingredients, if any.

*Avoid warped pie shells* by remembering to add enough prebaking fork pricks and to inspect the pie after five minutes of baking to see if any blisters have appeared that have to be pricked while baking.

*Slouching pie shells* are a sign of one of two omissions: flutes may not have been pressed to plate firmly enough, or pie has not been chilled for a half hour before baking.

### HOW TO FREEZE—HOW TO THAW

*Frozen unbaked pie shell.* Leave shell in pie plate. (Bake it in a metal-edged paper freezer pie plate so you don't tie up your regular baking equipment.) Freeze shells, properly wrapped for freezing, one at a time. Later stack frozen shells, separated by paddings of crumpled waxed paper, over-wrapped with moisture-vaporproof material.

*How to freeze baked pie shell.* Cool baked shell at room temperature. Freeze, then wrap. Store with or without pie plate. Stack in freezer, if you have several, well wrapped during storage.

*How to thaw that frozen unbaked pie shell.* Unwrap. Bake at 450°F. for 5 minutes. Prick again, if necessary, and bake 15 minutes longer. Or allow shell to remain wrapped at room temperature for half hour. Then bake 5 minutes, check for further pricking, and bake another 7 minutes.

*How to thaw frozen baked pie shell.* Unwrap, heat at

375°F. for 10 minutes, or until thawed. Or leave on wrapping and thaw at room temperature.

## NON-FREEZER STORAGE

*Two-day-old fruit pies* taste oven-fresh if stored in the refrigerator and reheated at 350°F. for 7 to 10 minutes before serving. Pies just brought home from the bakery are also restored to original oven-fresh flavor if heated for about 3 minutes before serving.

*Pie shells may be made in advance* of baking and stored by covering with foil or waxed paper and refrigerated for 2 or 3 days. Or bake pie shells in advance of filling and store, covered; then reheat for 5 minutes at 425°F.

*Pie, unless served fresh-from-the-oven warm,* must be kept cold. If you don't serve it right after baking, store it in the refrigerator.

## THE BREAKFAST NOOK

*Double-acting baking powder is a time-saver.* When used in preparing waffle or griddle-cake batter, mixture can be made ahead of time and stored several hours in refrigerator, because powder releases only about one third of its leavening action when cold, remaining two thirds during baking process.

*Waffles won't stick* to grids after this procedure: Clean grids with baking soda. Apply soda with stiff, wire-bristled brush. Removes all discoloration.

*Easy way to keep pancakes from sticking.* Fill small cheesecloth bag with table salt. Just before pouring batter, rub salt bag over surface of hot skillet or griddle. Not only keeps batter from sticking, but does away with need to grease utensil.

*For extra-tasty pancakes,* add a tablespoon of pancake syrup to the batter.

*Good breakfasts can be made quickly* if dry ingredients for muffins or pancakes are mixed the night before (and muffin tins greased).

# CAKE CREATIONS

*Mixes are time- and money-savers.* Follow package directions and you'll bake a perfect cake every time.

*If you mix your own,* start with a sound recipe from a reliable tested source. Follow it exactly, without making changes or substitutions, unless you have made a particular recipe often enough to risk experimenting.

*Have standard measuring equipment* and use it scrupulously, accurately. Never guess. Measure.

*Important measuring tools.* Two measuring cups (one for dry ingredients, the other for liquids) and one or two sets of measuring spoons are basic when you bake.

*In measuring flour,* remember it has a tendency to pack. To avoid using more than is necessary, sift flour before measuring. Lift sifted flour lightly by spoonfuls into cup, level off by drawing edge of spatula or flat knife across top. Never press flour or shake it down in cup.

*Measure baking powder carefully.* Even a small amount too much or too little can give disappointing results. Use dry standard measuring spoon. Dip spoon into baking powder, then level off lightly with edge of spatula or straight knife.

*Ways to measure shortening.* Press into measuring cup or tablespoon and pack lightly, scraping top flat with a spatula or straight knife. Another method is by water displacement.

To measure ½ cup shortening, for example, first half fill cup with water. Add shortening by spoonful until water rises to the top of cup. Then drain off water.

*In measuring butter*, allow ½ pound for 1 cup. Melted butter or shortening is measured like any liquid.

### MAKE LIKE AN EXPERT

*Know the role* of the different flours in cake baking.

*All-purpose flour* is used for pastries, biscuits, and breads, and for cakes that require moist, sturdy texture.

*Self-rising flour* contains leavening and salt and should be used only as per the instructions on the package.

*Special bread flour* is just that and nothing else, so must never be used in baking cake.

*As a general rule*, where a recipe specifies the kind of flour you are to use, use it.

*Storing rule.* To keep cake flour, close package flap securely after use and store in cool, dry place.

*"Keep your (baking) powder dry,"* too, as well as tightly closed and in a cool place. Long storage may reduce its strength too; better date the can so you may know when you bought it and replace if it's been on your pantry shelf for a year or more.

*Let the pan fit the cake.* For best results, cake batter should only half fill the pan.

*Warped pans* may cause batter to run to one side of pan and spoil not only appearance but also the quality of the finished product.

*Metal pans of light materials* are generally best for cakes. They heat quickly, yet reflect heat so that cakes brown delicately.

*If cake pan is too shallow*, you can build up the sides by lining with a "collar" or strip of heavy brown paper. Paper should be smoothed against greased sides of pan, then the paper itself well greased.

*For attractive layer cakes.* Insure uniform layers by using straight-sided pans and, if you're a true perfectionist, weighing batter, spooning it into each pan until weights are equal. A household scale works with you on this tip.

*If you want to bake special-shaped cakes* for festive occasions, yet haven't the space to store a lot of special-occasion cake pans, try shaping cake "pans" out of aluminum foil. Using heavy foil double, you can mold it into a heart for an engagement party, a Christmas tree for the Yule season, a star for the Fourth of July, and so on.

*Bake 'em oblong, shape 'em later.* Another way to have fancy cake shapes is to bake sheet cakes, cut paper patterns in the desired shape, lay the pattern on the cake, and carefully cut cake, using a hot knife, by following the edge of the pattern as you cut. Use leftover pieces of cake for *petits fours* and in cake-base desserts.

*Prepare the oven for baking.* Place racks where heat is most even, so baked product will rise evenly and brown perfectly. Start heating oven early enough before baking so you have even heat of the right temperature.

*Don't crowd your oven.* Never try to bake too much at once or place pans too close to oven wall. Heat must circulate freely on all sides of baking pan to give evenly baked results. When using two racks at the same time, do not place one pan directly over the other but stagger them on each rack.

*Special note for angel-food and sponge cakes.* Never grease the pan. These batters need to cling to sides of pan to reach full height. Batter, made up largely of beaten egg whites, is too delicate to hold up and give cake its full volume without support of sides of ungreased pan, to which cake clings during baking and cooling (in inverted pan). Greasing would cause such cakes to fall out of inverted pan while cooling, thus making them flat and soggy.

*"Life preserver" for sinking fruits and nuts.* If you heat them in the oven, then dust with flour, before adding to cake batter, fruits and nuts won't go to the bottom of the pan.

*To get perfectly shaped cupcakes,* grease just the bottom of cupcake cups. This helps keep cupcakes from running over. Or buy packaged paper liners. Then you'll have no greasing or scouring to do, no rough edges, and no chance of cake's sticking. Never fill cups more than half full. Cup from graduated set is good for pouring batter. So is a small soup ladle.

### CROWNING GLORIES

*Cooked cake frostings spread smoother* if you cool cake thoroughly before frosting. Then brush off all loose crumbs and trim off ragged edges.

*Hints on tints.* To tint frostings, add vegetable coloring, a few drops at a time, and mix frosting until evenly tinted.

*When using pastry bag,* fill only half full of frosting at a time for best results. Use one hand to guide tip and other to force frosting out gently. If in doubt about results, practice first on a piece of waxed paper.

*Make your own pastry bags.*

1. Paper. Cut rectangle, 10 inches by 8 inches, of sturdy waxed paper or thin parchment paper. Cut rectangle diagonally into two triangles. Roll each into cone, shape and fold down top points of cone to hold in place. Snip off top of cone to provide small opening.

2. Cloth. Shape bag from muslin or light canvas, then stitch. Metal tips of varying sizes and patterns can be inserted at bottom of either cloth or paper cone.

*To keep top from tipping.* If the top layer begins to slide when you frost a cake, insert wire cake tester or thin knitting needle through both layers to keep top layer in position. Remove wire or needle before frosting top layer. Or else leave it in until frosting is set, then cover mark with cake decoration.

*Very special cakes.* It pays to frost smoothly first with a thin layer of frosting, to hold down any crumbs and to give an even base coat. When set or firm, the final frosting will spread more evenly and easily.

*New use for toothpicks.* When trimming cake frosting, use toothpick to trace design lightly. Then apply trimming, such as tiny candies, nuts, melted jelly.

For *"different"* cake toppings, after the cake is frosted add such extra touches as chopped nuts, shredded coconut or cocoa sprinkled around a cardboard pattern or through a paper doily over a white frosting, vanilla sugar on dark frosting.

*Fresh flowers on your cake.* Sounds incredible? It can be done and creates an unusual and festive touch. Place small flowers in a small vase and insert into center of a tube cake (angel-food, sponge, etc.).

### TIME-SAVERS AND STORAGE TIPS

*Melt chocolate the easy way.* Grease the pan in which you melt chocolate; makes dishwashing easy afterward. Or melt chocolate in little cup made out of two thicknesses of aluminum foil.

*Cakes take to freezing.* You may bake your cake ahead of time for parties or box lunches, or for the unexpected guests for whom, "if you'd known they were coming, you'd have baked a cake."

*Frost cake before freezing,* if you wish, but remember not all frostings freeze well. If saving time is your motive and you must frost before freezing, don't use seven-minute or egg-type frostings; they become rubbery when frozen.

*Frozen cakes* will thaw rapidly at room temperature. For best eating quality, they should be served the day you thaw them.

*Always refrigerate* whipped-cream-frosted cakes, cream-filled cakes, or puff pastries.

### THE ART OF CAKE CUTTING

*Use long, sharp knife* in cutting cake to be sure you don't spoil its looks. If cake is frosted, rinse knife in hot water before using. Cut with gentle, sawing motion. Do not press down.

*For sponge cake or angel food,* cut lightly with very sharp or serrated knife, or gently "tear" off each piece, using two forks or a cake breaker.

# PAMPER THE FAMILY SWEET TOOTH

### "QUICKIE" DESSERTS—ICE CREAM SENSATIONS

*Go easy on sugar* when you make refrigerator desserts. Too much sugar prevents proper freezing.

*If brown sugar has hardened,* rub the solid chunk of sugar back and forth against a kitchen grater placed over a bowl. A kitchen sieve does the trick too.

*Best way to measure syrups.* Thick liquids and syrups (molasses, honey, etc.) should be poured into a measuring cup or spoon from their original containers. If cup has already been used to measure shortening or water, syrup will empty out readily. Don't dip measuring spoon into sticky liquids, for too much will cling to the underside of the spoon, causing overmeasurement or waste.

*Measure molasses the easy way.* First dip measuring cup full of flour. Empty it back into flour sack (or tin) and you leave a coating that prevents molasses from sticking to the glass. Every drop comes out cleanly.

### "SHORT-ORDER" DESSERTS AND TRIMMINGS

*Always-fresh doughnuts.* To recapture that "just-out-of-the-kettle" flavor of plain cake doughnuts, place them in a covered casserole and bake at 400°F., for five minutes. For an added touch of spice that's nice, roll them immediately afterward in sugar-cinnamon mixture.

*Gingerbread as an emergency dessert.* Keep a package of gingerbread mix on hand and you'll never be caught empty-handed, come dessert time, when you have these topping ideas:

1. Canned crushed pineapple and whipped cream.
2. Ice cream covered with chocolate sauce.
3. Custard sauce and grated orange rind.
4. Mincemeat folded into whipped cream.
5. Lemon sauce with nutmeg.
6. Applesauce sprinkled with sugar and cinnamon, poured on gingerbread, and placed under broiler until sauce bubbles.

*Modern angel cake* is heaven-sent, quick, delicious, and easy to make from a packaged angel-cake mix, or fresh from the freezer. For an unusual frosting, add instant-coffee powder to heavy cream, and whip. Sweeten to taste. For chocolate flavor, add instant cocoa.

*Marbled marvel in tapioca.* Prepare tapioca cream as directed on package, then spoon it into tall glasses. Between spoonfuls, add marbling layers such as: Melted semi-sweet chocolate and chopped nuts, syrupy melted brown sugar and butter, melted currant jelly tossed with coconut, or baby-pack strained peaches flavored with almond.

### PUTTING PUDDING ON THE SOCIETY PAGE

*Cornstarch pudding* goes elegant when you make it into black-on-black chocolate pudding by adding a square of melted chocolate. Serve warm, with chocolate ice cream on top.

*Dream pudding* is simply cornstarch pudding chilled, then beaten with an egg beater, and ½ cup whipped heavy cream folded in. Flavor with a dash of almond or rum extract.

*Fanciful custards.* To make rennet custard, add teaspoon of sherry. To chocolate custard, add instant coffee powder, then rum extract. To chocolate custard, add almond extract for exotic flavor.

*No-bake custard.* Packaged custard-dessert mix cooks in about seven minutes, and you cannot tell it from the baked thing in a million years.

## AWAY AND WAYS WITH COOKIES

*When sending home-baked cookies* to camp or school, aluminum-foil packing is a smart idea. Being greaseproof, odorproof, and moistureproof, foil insures that the cookies (or cake) arrive in perfect condition, moist and fresh. And, since aluminum is in the nature of a soft suit of armor, your baking will arrive unbroken and uncrushed if packed right, with air spaces properly filled.

*Storage.* Airtight, cold, or freezing. Store crisp cookies in a container with a loose-fitting cover. To recrisp in humid weather, place cookies in an open shallow pan in a 300°F. oven for three to five minutes.

*Empty butter cartons* are fine for molding and storing cookie dough in the refrigerator. The cartons come waxed so they need no greasing. In addition, when the dough is sliced for cookies, each will be uniform in size.

## ICE-CREAM SENSATIONS THAT ARE EASY TO CREATE

*Flaming mincemeat.* Spoon heated prepared mincemeat on that vanilla or coffee ice cream. Top with cube of sugar dipped into lemon or rum extract, then light a match to it. Real "continental," no?

*Snowballs.* Roll balls of ice cream in shredded coconut or chopped nuts. Serve on top of a serving of chocolate sauce or pour canned crushed fruit sauce over balls.

*Ice-cream cookie sandwich.* A favorite among young fry. From cylinder container, slice ice cream ½-inch thick. Place slices between large sugar cookies or wafers, sandwich-fashion.

*Don't give pie à la mode monopoly.* Other desserts that are special and delicious with ice-cream topping include hot gingerbread, chocolate or butterscotch pudding, Dutch apple or plum cake, bread pudding, fruit cobblers, fruit Betties, toasted sponge cake or angel cake slices, cold brownies, shortcakes, fruit tarts, Indian pudding, honeydew or cantaloupe.

*Your "sundae best."* Actually, a sundae consists of ice cream, sauce, whipped cream, and a cherry. But many shortcut sundaes can be made with a fancy topping. For instance:

*Peanut pebbles.* Crushed peanut brittle over chocolate, coffee, or vanilla ice cream.

*Cherry plus.* Crushed Bing cherries and syrup over strawberry ice cream.

*Almond supreme.* Pistachio ice cream topped with chocolate sauce and whole salted toasted blanched almonds, the nuts still warm from the toasting.

*Brazil delight.* Coffee ice cream sprinkled generously with chocolate and Brazil-nut shavings. Add a little shredded coconut too, if you like.

### IDEAS THAT MAKE YOU A WIZARD TO YOUR CHILDREN

*Malt topping.* Sprinkle cocoa or chocolate-flavored malted-milk powder over ice cream, with or without chocolate sauce. (Most youngsters will vote, "with" on the sauce.)

*Clown cone.* On large chocolate cookie or chocolate-covered doughnut place a round ball of vanilla ice cream, topped with inverted cone wafer hat. Make a face on the ice cream, using chocolate candy bits for eyes and nose, and a snipped maraschino cherry for the mouth.

*A-B-C block.* Cut square block of ice cream, etch edg-

ings and letters in whipped cream with tube of cake deco-
ator.

*Potted heart.* Plant a red, heart-shaped lollipop in a fluted,
colored party cup filled with chocolate ice cream. For the
leaves, use long green gumdrops, sliced lengthwise.

*Snow man.* Top a large vanilla ice-cream ball with a
smaller one, both rolled in shredded coconut. For eyes and
buttons, raisins. For mouth, a cherry. For the hat, an inverted paper party cup. For the broom, a lollipop.

### TREAT IT GENTLY

*Ice cream is sensitive.* It loses most of its velvety texture
if handled too much. The richer the cream, the colder is
the freezing and storing temperature it requires, especially
for long storage. Ice-cream desserts need low temperatures
even more. Unless stored at zero, freezer temperature, don't
keep ice cream longer than a few hours.

*Who wants to wait for ice cream?* When the ice-cream
carton is hard to pull off, just cut through the rim with a
knife and your ice cream is ready to serve.

*Ice cream is good for a month* in your home freezer, if
you follow the instructions you received with your freezer
on storing ice cream.

*In refrigerator-freezer combinations* the normal freezer setting is at zero, just right for storing ice-cream desserts hours
ahead. The freezer part of the combination can be set at
coldest point without affecting the temperature of the refrigerator itself.

# YOUR CALORIE COUNTER

*Consult your doctor* before starting any diet program, whether yours is a losing or weight-gaining problem.

*If you are underweight,* don't try to change your diet habits suddenly, or you'll become quickly discouraged. Gradually add extra-fattening foods daily, and start drinking midmorning and midafternoon milkshakes. An important factor is to allow for a relaxation period as often during the day, especially after meals, as you can make time for.

*As you battle your bulges,* remember that the more you avoid carbohydrates like sugar and starches (and alcohol) the more of your stored-up fat is used up by your body and eliminated. Limit your carbohydrates to a minimum, in the bread and potato department since both of those foods are highly nutritious. (It only takes a few minutes to eat a rich dessert like pie à la mode but oh, how long to get rid of the layer it leaves where you need it least.)

*Calorie content of family foods* can only be approximated because many dishes contain a combination of low and high calorie ingredients. For weight losers, however, the calorie counter is a guide on foods to use sparingly or to avoid, always working under your doctor's guidance. And weight gainers have lots of delicious foods to select from those that are loaded with calories.

*Family food-portion sizes vary too,* according to energy

expended on work and play. And no one member of your family may take exactly the ½-cup portions often listed in the calorie counter as containing a certain number of calories.

*What you put into salads*, how much you eat of them, and how much dressing you use, determine whether they are for weight gainers or losers. Here are some salad combinations:

| FOOD | APPROXIMATE MEASURE | CALORIES |
|---|---|---|
| Apple and carrot with mayonnaise | ½ cup on lettuce | 100 |
| Avocado with tomato, cheese, French dressing | lettuce, ¼ pear, ½ tomato, 2 T. cheese, 1 T. dressing | 245 |
| Banana, nuts, with mayonnaise | lettuce, ½ banana, 1 T. walnuts, 1 T. mayonnaise | 260 |
| Banana, orange, mayonnaise | lettuce, ½ banana, ½ orange, 1 T. mayonnaise | 195 |
| Cabbage, apple, mayonnaise | lettuce, ½ c. chopped cabbage, ¼ large apple, 1 T. mayonnaise | 150 |
| Carrot, orange, lemon juice | lettuce, ½ c. fruit and carrot, cut-up; lemon juice to taste | 50 |
| Chicken, celery, mayonnaise | lettuce, ½ cup filling | 250 |
| Crab, celery, mayonnaise | lettuce, ½ cup filling | 175 |
| Cream cheese, pineapple, dressing | lettuce, 1 slice pineapple, 2 T. cheese, 1 T. dressing | 200 |
| Egg, tomato, mayonnaise | lettuce, ½ sliced tomato, ½ egg, 1 T. dressing | 150 |
| Mixed greens with French dressing | ½ cup greens, 1 T. dressing | 50–60 |
| Orange, grapefruit, fruit salad dressing | lettuce, 2 slices orange, 3 sections grapefruit, 1 T. dressing | 150 |
| Jellied vegetable, no dressing | lettuce, ½ cup salad | 40 |
| Potato salad, mayonnaise | lettuce, ½ cup filling | 200 |
| Prune, cottage cheese, mayonnaise | lettuce, 4 prunes, 2 T. cheese | 200 |
| Salmon, celery, mayonnaise | lettuce, ½ cup filling | 195 |
| Tomato, lettuce, no dressing | lettuce, 1 small tomato | 30 |
| Tomato jelly, no dressing | lettuce, ½ cup jelly | 35 |
| Tuna, celery, mayonnaise | lettuce, ½ cup filling | 200 |

# *BREADS, BISCUITS, ROLLS, ETC.

| FOOD | APPROXIMATE MEASURE | CALORIES |
|---|---|---|
| Waldorf, mayonnaise | lettuce, ½ cup filling | 185 |
| Biscuits and buns | 1 average size | 100–109 |
| Boston brown | thin to average slice | 71–89 |
| Bran bread | 1 slice | 75 |
| Bread stuffing | ½ cup | 233 |
| Corn bread | average piece | 100–139 |
| Corn stick | 1 average | 128 |
| Date and nut bread | average slice | 85–100 |
| Danish pastry | 1 small | 139 |
| French bread | 1 small slice | 50–54 |
| Griddle cake | 5-inch round | 100 |
| Hard roll | 1 average | 90 |
| Melba toast | 3 slices | 75 |
| Muffins | 1 average | 106–120 |
| Popover | 3-inch round | 60–90 |
| Raisin bran bread | average slice | 148 |
| Raisin bread | thin to average slice | 65–100 |
| Rye bread | thin to average slice | 57–70 |
| Soft roll | 1 average | 81–122 |
| Vienna bread | average slice | 128 |
| White bread | thin to average slice | 55–80 |
| White sweet roll | 1 average | 178 |

## CRACKERS, ETC.

| | | |
|---|---|---|
| Cheese | 3–4 small | 100 |
| Graham | 2 pieces | 80–100 |
| Oatmeal | 1 piece | 35–39 |
| Pretzels | 5 pieces | 35–100 |
| Rusk | 1 piece | 50 |
| Rye Krisp | 2 pieces | 50 |
| Saltines | 2 pieces | 50 |
| Soda | 2 pieces | 50 |
| Zwiebach | 3 slices | 100 |

## CEREALS

| | | |
|---|---|---|
| Bran flakes | ⅔ cup | 97–100 |
| Corn flakes | 1 cup | 109–125 |
| Cream of wheat | ¾ cup | 110–125 |
| Farina | ½ cup | 70–80 |
| Grape nuts | ½ cup | 180–200 |
| Hominy grits | ⅔ cup | 100–125 |
| Krispies | ⅔ cup | 100 |
| Oatmeal | ⅔ cup | 100–125 |
| Puffed rice | ⅔ cup | 50 |
| Puffed wheat | ⅔ cup | 50–75 |
| Shredded wheat | 1 large | 100 |

* Allows for no butter or other spread.

| FOOD | APPROXIMATE MEASURE | CALORIES |
|---|---|---|
| Triscuits | 3 pieces | 100–105 |
| Wheatena | ⅔ cup | 100 |
| Wheat flakes | ⅔ cup | 100 |

## CONDIMENTS AND SAUCES
### (SEE ALSO FATS AND OILS)

| | | |
|---|---|---|
| A-1 sauce | 1 tablespoon | 10 |
| Apple butter | 1 tablespoon | 75 |
| Catsup | 1 tablespoon | 15–25 |
| Cherry sauce | 1 tablespoon | 10–25 |
| Chili sauce | 1 tablespoon | 50–100 |
| Chocolate cornstarch | 1 tablespoon | 50 |
| Cranberry jelly or sauce | 1 tablespoon | 100 |
| Cream sauce | 4 tablespoons | 100 |
| French dressing | 1 tablespoon | 50 |
| Creole sauce | 1 tablespoon | 50–100 |
| Fruit jellies | 1 tablespoon | 50 |
| Gravy (thick) | 2 tablespoons | 75–100 |
| Gravy (thin) | 2 tablespoons | 40–75 |
| Hollandaise sauce | 1 tablespoon | 50 |
| Horseradish | 1 teaspoon | 5 |
| Jam | 1 tablespoon | 50 |
| Lemon sauce | 1 tablespoon | 25 |
| Marmalade | 1 tablespoon | 50 |
| Mayonnaise | 1 tablespoon | 100 |
| Miracle whip | 1 tablespoon | 50 |
| Mustard | 1 teaspoon | 5–10 |
| Olives (green) | 12 medium (unstuffed) | 100 |
| Olives (ripe) | 8–10 medium | 75–100 |
| Olive oil | 1 tablespoon | 100 |
| Peanut butter | 1 tablespoon | 100 |
| Pepper (green) | 1, 3 inches long | 0–20 |
| Pickles (dill) | 1 medium | 5 |
| Pickles (sweet) | 1 small | 10 |
| Preserves | 1 tablespoon | 50 |
| Roquefort dressing | 1 tablespoon | 100 |
| Russian dressing | 1 tablespoon | 50–100 |
| Tartare sauce | 1 tablespoon | 100 |
| Thousand Island dressing | 1 tablespoon | 75 |
| Tomato sauce | 1 tablespoon | 5–25 |
| Vinegar | 1 tablespoon | None |
| White sauce | 4 tablespoons | 100 |
| Wine sauce | 3 tablespoons | 60 |
| Worcestershire sauce | 1 teaspoon | 10 |

## DAIRY PRODUCTS

| | | |
|---|---|---|
| American cheese (Cheddar) | 1 ounce | 79–100 |
| Brie cheese | 1 ounce | 100 |

| FOOD | APPROXIMATE MEASURE | CALORIES |
|---|---|---|
| Buttermilk | 8-ounce glass | 85–100 |
| Butter | 1 tablespoon | 100 |
| Camembert cheese | 1 ounce | 100–150 |
| Cottage cheese | 1 tablespoon | 10–20 |
| Cream cheese | 1 tablespoon | 50 |
| Cream (light, 30%) | 1 tablespoon | 25 |
| Cream (whipping, 40%) | 1 tablespoon | 50 |
| Cream (sour, 30%) | 1 tablespoon | 25 |
| Condensed milk (sweetened) | 1 tablespoon | 66–75 |
| Condensed milk (unsweetened) | 1 tablespoon | 20–35 |
| Edam cheese | 1 ounce | 100 |
| Evaporated milk | 2 tablespoons | 25–35 |
| Head cheese | 1½ ounces | 100 |
| Liederkranz cheese | 1 ounce | 200 |
| Limburger | 1 ounce | 100 |
| Milk (fresh, whole) | 8-ounce glass | 166–168 |
| Milk, (fresh, skimmed) | 8-ounce glass | 86–87 |
| Parmesan cheese (grated) | 1 tablespoon | 25–35 |
| Pot cheese | 1 tablespoon | 25 |
| Roquefort cheese | 1 sector | 100–150 |
| Swiss cheese | 1 ounce | 100 |
| Swiss Gruyère cheese | 1 ounce | 100 |

## EGGS

| | | |
|---|---|---|
| Boiled | 1 medium | 70–75 |
| Deviled (mayonnaise) | 1 medium | 100 |
| Fried | 1 medium | 100 |
| Eggnog | 1 medium | 230 |
| Omelet | 1 medium | 105–125 |
| Poached | 1 medium | 70–75 |
| Scrambled | 1 medium | 135–200 |
| Egg white only | 1 egg | 15 |
| Egg yolk only | 1 egg | 55–60 |

## FATS AND OILS

| | | |
|---|---|---|
| Bacon | 1 tablespoon | 100 |
| Butter | 1 tablespoon | 100 |
| Chicken fat | 1 tablespoon | 100 |
| Cod liver oil | 1 tablespoon | 100 |
| Cotton seed oil | 1 tablespoon | 100 |
| Cream dressing | 1 tablespoon | 50 |
| Crisco | 1 tablespoon | 100 |
| French dressing | 1 tablespoon | 50 |
| Lard | 1 tablespoon | 100 |
| Mayonnaise | 1 tablespoon | 100 |
| Mineral oil | 1 tablespoon | None |
| Oleomargarine | 1 tablespoon | 100 |
| Olive oil | 1 tablespoon | 100 |
| Peanut butter | 1 tablespoon | 100 |

| FOOD | APPROXIMATE MEASURE | CALORIES |
|---|---|---|
| Roquefort dressing | 1 tablespoon | 100 |
| Russian dressing | 1 tablespoon | 75–80 |
| Thousand Island dressing | 1 tablespoon | 100 |

## FLOUR FOODS

| | | |
|---|---|---|
| Buckwheat cakes | 6-inch diameter | 150 |
| Dumplings | 1 medium | 100 |
| Macaroni (with cheese) | 1 cup | 175–300 |
| Noodles (cooked) | ¾ cup | 100 |
| Pancakes (French) | 6-inch diameter | 200 |
| Pancakes (plain) | 6-inch diameter | 100–125 |
| Spaghetti (canned) | 1 cup | 250–300 |
| Spaghetti (cooked) | 1 cup | 200 |
| Spanish rice | 1 cup | 300 |
| Waffles | 5-inch diameter or square | 200–252 |
| Wheat cakes | 6-inch diameter | 150 |

## FRUITS

| | | |
|---|---|---|
| Apple | 1 medium | 75–100 |
| Apple (baked) | 1 medium | 100–150 |
| Applesauce | ½ cup | 100–135 |
| Apricot (fresh) | 1 medium | 20–25 |
| Apricot (canned) | 4 medium | 100 |
| Apricot (dried) | 10 halves | 100 |
| Apricot (stewed) | 10 halves | 125–200 |
| Avocado | ½ medium | 200–250 |
| Banana | 1 medium | 100–125 |
| Blackberries (fresh) | ½ cup | 50 |
| Blackberries (canned) | ½ cup | 100 |
| Blueberries (fresh) | ½ cup | 50 |
| Blueberries (canned) | ½ cup | 100 |
| Cantaloupe | ½ medium | 50 |
| Cherries (fresh) | 1 cup | 100 |
| Crab apples | each | 50 |
| Cranberries | ½ cup | 100 |
| Dates | each | 25 |
| Figs (fresh) | each | 35 |
| Grapes | ½ cup | 100 |
| Grapefruit | ½ medium | 75 |
| Huckleberries | ½ cup | 75 |
| Lemons | 1 medium | 25 |
| Loganberries (fresh) | ¾ cup | 100 |
| Melon (honeydew) | ¼ piece | 75 |
| Nectarines | 1 medium | 75 |
| Orange | 1 medium | 75–80 |
| Peaches (canned) | 2 halves | 100 |
| Peach (fresh) | 1 medium | 35 |
| Pears (canned) | 3 halves | 100 |

| FOOD | APPROXIMATE MEASURE | CALORIES |
|---|---|---|
| Pear (fresh) | 1 medium | 50 |
| Persimmons | 1 medium | 100 |
| Pineapple (canned) | 2 slices | 100 |
| Pineapple (fresh) | 1 slice | 50 |
| Pineapple (crushed) | ½ cup | 200 |
| Plum (fresh) | 1 medium | 20 |
| Pomegranate | 1 medium | 75 |
| Prunes (dried) | 5 medium | 100 |
| Prunes (stewed) | 5 medium | 200 |
| Raisins | ¼ cup | 125 |
| Raspberries (fresh) | ½ cup | 50 |
| Rhubarb (canned) | ½ cup | 75 |
| Strawberries (fresh) | 1 cup | 100 |
| Tangerines | 1 medium | 25 |
| Tomatoes (raw) | 1 medium | 25 |
| Watermelon | 1 slice | 100 |

## FRUIT JUICES AND OTHERS

| | | |
|---|---|---|
| Apple | 1 4-ounce glass | 100 |
| Carrot | 1 4-ounce glass | 25 |
| Clam | 1 4-ounce glass | 75 |
| Grape | 1 4-ounce glass | 75 |
| Grapefruit | 1 4-ounce glass | 75 |
| Kraut | 1 4-ounce glass | 25 |
| Lemon | 1 4-ounce glass | 25 |
| Lime | 1 4-ounce glass | 75 |
| Orange | 1 4-ounce glass | 75 |
| Pineapple | 1 4-ounce glass | 100 |
| Prune | 1 4-ounce glass | 200 |
| Tomato | 1 4-ounce glass | 35 |

## SOUPS AND BROTHS

| | | |
|---|---|---|
| Asparagus (creamed) | ¾ cup | 200 |
| Bean (navy) | ¾ cup | 200 |
| Beef | ¾ cup | 75 |
| Bouillon | ¾ cup | 0–10 |
| Celery (creamed) | ¾ cup | 200 |
| Chicken broth | ¾ cup | 50 |
| Chicken gumbo | ¾ cup | 150 |
| Chicken noodle | ¾ cup | 100–150 |
| Chicken with rice | ¾ cup | 100–150 |
| Clam chowder | ¾ cup | 150 |
| Consommé | ¾ cup | 35 |
| Corn (creamed, chowder) | ¾ cup | 200 |
| Lentil | ¾ cup | 200 |
| Mock turtle | ¾ cup | 200 |
| Mushroom (creamed) | ¾ cup | 200 |
| Onion (French) | ¾ cup | 125 |
| Oxtail | ¾ cup | 150 |

| FOOD | APPROXIMATE MEASURE | CALORIES |
|---|---|---|
| Oyster (creamed) | ¾ cup | 250 |
| Pea (creamed) | ¾ cup | 200 |
| Pea (dried, split) | ¾ cup | 150 |
| Potato (creamed) | ¾ cup | 200–250 |
| Scotch broth | ¾ cup | 100 |
| Spinach (creamed) | ¾ cup | 200 |
| Tomato | ¾ cup | 75 |
| Tomato (creamed) | ¾ cup | 200 |
| Vegetable | ¾ cup | 85–150 |
| Vegetable and beef | ¾ cup | 150–200 |

## MEATS
### (When fried, add calorie content of Fats and Oils)

| FOOD | APPROXIMATE MEASURE | CALORIES |
|---|---|---|
| Bacon | 3–4 slices | 100 |
| Beef (corned-hashed) | ½ cup | 100 |
| Beef (hamburger) | medium patty | 200 |
| Beef (kidney) | 1 whole | 250 |
| Beef (liver) | medium slice | 100 |
| Beef (pot roast) | medium slice | 100 |
| Beef (rib roast) | medium slice | 100 |
| Beef (sirloin steak) | medium slice | 100 |
| Beef (stew) | 1 cup | 250 |
| Beef (sweetbreads) | ½ cup | 100 |
| Beef (tenderloin) | medium piece | 300 |
| Beef (tongue) | 2 ounces | 130 |
| Brains (calves) | ¾ cup | 100 |
| Frankfurters | medium size | 100 |
| Ham (smoked) | medium slice | 250 |
| Lamb chop (broiled, lean) | medium size | 100 |
| Lamb roast | medium slice | 100 |
| Meat balls | 1 medium | 100 |
| Meat loaf | medium slice | 100 |
| Pigs' feet (pickled) | small piece | 75 |
| Pork chop (lean meat) | medium size | 200 |
| Pork spareribs | 4 rib pieces | 150 |
| Pork tenderloin | 1 piece | 225 |
| Sausage (bologna) | 1½ ounces | 100 |
| Sausage (liverwurst) | medium slice | 70–75 |
| Sausage (pork) | medium size | 50–60 |
| Sausage (salami) | medium slice | 50 |
| Sweetbreads (broiled) | ½ pair | 175 |
| Veal cutlet (breaded) | medium piece | 150–280 |
| Veal liver (fried) | medium piece | 200 |
| Veal (roast) | medium slice | 100 |
| Veal (steak) | medium piece | 100 |
| Veal (stew) | 1 cup | 200 |
| Venison | medium slice | 125 |
| Wiener schnitzel | medium slice | 250 |

## MISCELLANEOUS

| FOOD | APPROXIMATE MEASURE | CALORIES |
|------|---------------------|----------|
| Chop suey | ½ cup | 250 |
| Chow mein | ½ cup | 150 |
| Con carne (chili) | ½ cup | 150 |
| Egg roll | 1 piece | 150 |
| Gelatin (unflavored) | 1 tablespoon | 25–35 |
| Hungarian goulash | 1 cup | 300 |
| Rabbit | per ½ pound | 250–400 |
| Vinegar | 1 tablespoon | None |
| Yeast (dried) | 1 tablespoon | 25 |

## FISH, SEAFOODS

| | | |
|------|---------------------|----------|
| Abalone | 4 ounces | 100 |
| Bass | 4 ounces | 100 |
| Bluefish | 4 ounces | 100 |
| Caviar | 1 tablespoon | 100 |
| Clams (bluepoints, raw) | 6 medium | 75–100 |
| Clams (cherrystone) | 6 medium | 75–100 |
| Cod fish | 4 ounces | 100 |
| Cod fish cakes | 1 medium | 100–125 |
| Crab meat (canned) | ½ cup | 50–67 |
| Crab (cooked) | 1 medium | 75 |
| Crab (soft-shell) | 1 medium | 75 |
| Finnan haddie | 4 ounces | 100 |
| Flounder | 4 ounces | 100 |
| Frog legs | 2 medium | 75 |
| Gefuelte fish | ⅘ cup | 100 |
| Haddock | 4 ounces | 100 |
| Halibut | 4 ounces | 120–125 |
| Herring (pickled) | 4 ounces | 100 |
| Lobster (canned) | ½ cup | 75 |
| Lobster (fresh) | 1 medium | 150 |
| Mackerel (fresh) | 4 ounces | 100–125 |
| Mussels | 10 medium | 75 |
| Oysters (fried) | 4 medium | 325 |
| Oysters (raw) | 6 medium | 75–100 |
| Oyster stew (with milk) | 1 cup (4 oysters) | 250–270 |
| Perch | 4 ounces | 75 |
| Pike | 4 ounces | 75 |
| Red snapper | 4 ounces | 75 |
| Salmon (canned) | ½ cup | 100–150 |
| Salmon (fresh) | average slice | 200 |
| Sardines (canned in oil) | 1 can | 200 |
| Scallops (fried) | 4–6 medium | 225 |
| Shad | 4 ounces | 100 |
| Shadroe | average helping | 100 |
| Shrimp | 4 ounces | 100 |
| Smelts | 3 medium | 100 |

| FOOD | APPROXIMATE MEASURE | CALORIES |
|---|---|---|
| Sole | 4 ounces | 100 |
| Swordfish | 4 ounces | 100–150 |
| Trout (lake) | 4 ounces | 100–125 |
| Tuna (canned) | ½ cup | 155 |
| Tuna (fresh) | 4 ounces | 100 |
| Whitefish (broiled) | 4 ounces | 125 |

## POULTRY AND FOWL

| | | |
|---|---|---|
| Chicken (broiled) | ½ medium | 100 |
| Chicken (canned) | ¼ cup | 100 |
| Chicken (creamed) | ½ cup | 200 |
| Chicken (fried) | ½ small | 200 |
| Chicken (roasted) | 3 slices | 150–200 |
| Duck (roasted) | ¼ medium | 300 |
| Goose (roasted) | ⅛ medium | 300 |
| Pheasant (roasted) | ½ medium | 200 |
| Squab (roasted) | 1 medium | 200 |
| Turkey (roasted) | 2 slices | 200 |
| Turkey (white meat only) | 1 piece (4-inch square) | 100 |

## VEGETABLES

| | | |
|---|---|---|
| Artichokes (French or globe) | 1 medium | 75–100 |
| Artichokes (Jerusalem) | 5 medium | 100 |
| Artichokes (canned hearts) | 5 hearts | 50 |
| Asparagus | 5 spears | 10 |
| Bamboo shoots | ½ cup | 25 |
| Beans (baked, canned) | ½ cup | 150 |
| Beans (kidney, canned) | ½ cup | 300 |
| Beans (lima, fresh) | ½ cup | 100 |
| Beans (navy) | ½ cup | 150 |
| Beans (string or snap) | ½ cup | 12–15 |
| Beans (wax) | ½ cup | 12–15 |
| Beets (cooked) | ½ cup | 25 |
| Beet greens | ½ cup | 12–15 |
| Broccoli | ½ cup | 25 |
| Brussels sprouts | ½ cup | 25 |
| Cabbage (cooked) | ½ cup | 10 |
| Cabbage (raw) | ½ cup | 15 |
| Carrots (cooked) | ½ cup | 25 |
| Carrots (raw) | ½ cup | 25 |
| Cauliflower | 1 cup | 25 |
| Celery | 4 stalks | 10 |
| Chard | 1 cup | 25 |
| Chicory | 1 bunch | 5 |
| Collards | ½ cup | 12–15 |
| Corn (canned) | ½ cup | 100 |
| Corn on the cob | 1 ear | 100 |
| Cucumber | 1 medium | 10 |
| Dandelion greens | 1 cup | 25 |

| FOOD | APPROXIMATE MEASURE | CALORIES |
|---|---|---|
| Eggplant | 1 slice | 25 |
| Endive | 1 medium crown | 10–12 |
| Escarole | 1 heart | 10–12 |
| Kale | 1 cup | 25 |
| Kohlrabi | 1 cup | 50 |
| Leek | 1 piece | 10 |
| Lentils | ½ cup | 200 |
| Lettuce | medium head | 25 |
| Mushrooms | 1 cup | 0–10 |
| Mustard greens | 1 cup | 25 |
| Okra | ½ cup | 25 |
| Olives (green) | 12 medium | 100 |
| Olives (ripe) | 8–10 medium | 100 |
| Onions (white) | ½ cup | 50 |
| Parsley | 1 bunch | 5 |
| Parsnips | ½ cup | 50 |
| Peas (canned) | ½ cup | 100 |
| Peas (fresh or frozen) | ½ cup | 75 |
| Pepper | whole medium | 15 |
| Potato (baked, no butter) | 1 medium | 100–150 |
| Potato (French fried) | 5 pieces | 100 |
| Potato (hash browned) | ½ cup | 100 |
| Potato (mashed) | ½ cup | 100 |
| Potato (sweet) | 1 medium | 200 |
| Pumpkin | 1 cup | 100 |
| Radishes | 6 only | 15 |
| Rhubarb (fresh) | 1 cup | 25 |
| Rutabagas | ½ cup | 25 |
| Sauerkraut | 1 cup | 25 |
| Spinach | 1 cup | 25 |
| Squash (winter) | ½ cup | 50 |
| Squash (summer) | ½ cup | 25 |
| Succotash | ½ cup | 100 |
| Tomatoes (canned) | 1 cup | 50 |
| Tomatoes (raw) | 1 medium | 25 |
| Turnips (cooked) | ½ cup | 25 |
| Turnip tops | 1 cup | 25 |
| Water cress | 1 bunch | 10 |
| Yams | 1 medium | 200 |

## CAKES AND COOKIES

| | | |
|---|---|---|
| Angel food | 1 slice | 100 |
| Brownies | 2-inch square | 100 |
| Chocolate cookies | 1 piece | 100 |
| Chocolate layer cake | 1 slice | 300–400 |
| Chocolate marshmallow cookies | 1 piece | 150 |
| Coconut cake | 1 slice | 100 |
| Cup cake | 1 piece | 100 |
| Coffee cake | average piece | 200 |

| FOOD | APPROXIMATE MEASURE | CALORIES |
|---|---|---|
| Devil's food cake | 1 slice | 150–200 |
| Date cookies | 1 piece | 50–150 |
| Doughnuts (plain) | 1 medium | 200–300 |
| Doughnuts (sugared) | 1 medium | 300–375 |
| Doughnuts (French) | 1 medium | 350 |
| Fig newtons | 1 piece | 50–100 |
| Fruit cake | 1 slice | 100–350 |
| Gingersnaps | 1 piece | 25–50 |
| Gingerbread | 1 slice | 200 |
| Gingercake | 1 slice | 200–300 |
| Honey cookies | 1 piece | 50 |
| Icebox cookies | 1 piece | 50 |
| Lorna Doones | 1 piece | 35 |
| Macaroons (almond) | 1 piece | 50 |
| Macaroons (coconut) | 1 piece | 90–100 |
| Molasses cookies | 1 piece | 35 |
| Nabisco | 1 piece | 20 |
| Oatmeal cookies | 1 piece | 50–100 |
| Petits fours | 1 piece | 150 |
| Pound cake | 1 slice | 125–150 |
| Short cake | 1 serving | 250 |
| Sponge cake | 1 slice | 100–150 |
| Sugar cookies | 1 piece | 50 |
| Vanilla wafers | 1 piece | 25 |
| Waffles | 5-inch square or round | 200–250 |

## ICE CREAM AND ICES

| | | |
|---|---|---|
| Chocolate | 1 scoop | 250 |
| Chocolate sundae | 1 serving | 400 |
| Ices (all flavors) | 1 scoop | 75–100 |
| Marshmallow sundae | 1 serving | 400 |
| Nesselrode | 1 serving | 500 |
| Sodas (all flavors) | 1 10-ounce glass | 350 |
| Strawberry | 1 scoop | 200 |
| Strawberry sundae | 1 serving | 450 |
| Vanilla | 1 scoop | 100–150 |
| Walnut sundae | 1 serving | 450 |

## PASTRIES

| | | |
|---|---|---|
| Chocolate eclair | 1 medium | 175–200 |
| Cream puff | 1 medium | 175–200 |
| French pastry | 1 medium | 250 |
| Ladyfingers | 1 piece | 50 |
| Tarts | 1 piece | 100–200 |

## PIES (⅙ OF PIE, 12-INCH DIAMETER)

| | | |
|---|---|---|
| Apple | 1 piece | 300–350 |
| Apricot | 1 piece | 350 |

| FOOD | APPROXIMATE MEASURE | CALORIES |
|---|---|---|
| Banana cream | 1 piece | 350 |
| Berry (all) | 1 piece | 350 |
| Butterscotch | 1 piece | 350 |
| Cherry | 1 piece | 350 |
| Coconut custard | 1 piece | 350 |
| Lemon meringue | 1 piece | 250–350 |
| Mince | 1 piece | 400–450 |
| Peach | 1 piece | 350 |
| Pecan | 1 piece | 400–450 |
| Prune | 1 piece | 250–300 |
| Pumpkin | 1 piece | 200–275 |
| Raisin | 1 piece | 400–450 |
| Rhubarb | 1 piece | 270–350 |

## PUDDINGS AND DESSERTS

| | | |
|---|---|---|
| Apple dumpling | 1 medium | 300 |
| Apple snow | ½ cup | 75 |
| Apricot whip | ½ cup | 100 |
| Banana custard | ½ cup | 35–125 |
| Banana whip | ½ cup | 50–60 |
| Blanc mange (chocolate) | ½ cup | 200 |
| Bread pudding | ½ cup | 100 |
| Brown Betty | ½ cup | 150 |
| Cornstarch (all) | ½ cup | 200 |
| Custard (plain) | ½ cup | 125 |
| Custard (caramel) | ½ cup | 150 |
| Date pudding | ½ cup | 100–150 |
| Fig pudding | ½ cup | 100–150 |
| Floating island | ½ cup | 125 |
| Fruit gelatin | ½ cup | 50 |
| Gingerbread | 1 serving | 175 |
| Jello (all flavors) | ½ cup | 50 |
| Junket (all flavors) | ½ cup | 50 |
| Plum (no sauce) | ½ cup | 150 |
| Prune whip | ½ cup | 100 |
| Rice custard | ½ cup | 150 |
| Snow pudding | ½ cup | 125 |
| Tapioca | ½ cup | 120–150 |

## CANDIES

| | | |
|---|---|---|
| Caramel | 1 piece | 40–100 |
| Chocolate (plain) | small bar | 250–350 |
| Chocolate (with nuts) | small bar | 230–400 |
| Chocolate cream | small | 50–100 |
| Chocolate fudge | 1 square | 100–150 |
| Marshmallows | 5 pieces | 100–125 |
| Mints (cream) | 1 small piece | 25–35 |
| Nougat | 1 small piece | 50 |
| Peanut bar | 1 bar | 435 |

| FOOD | APPROXIMATE MEASURE | CALORIES |
|---|---|---|
| Praline | 1 3-inch piece | 300 |
| Sour balls | 1 piece | 20 |
| Taffy (salt water) | 1 piece | 75 |

## NUTS

| | | |
|---|---|---|
| Almonds (plain) | 12–15 nuts | 100 |
| Brazil nuts | 2 large | 100 |
| Butternuts | 4–5 nuts | 100 |
| Cashews | 4–5 nuts | 100 |
| Chestnuts (roasted) | 8 large | 100 |
| Chestnuts (shredded) | 3 tablespoons | 75–100 |
| Filberts or hazelnuts | 8–10 nuts | 100 |
| Hickory nuts | 12–15 nuts | 100 |
| Litchi nuts | 12 nuts | 100 |
| Peanuts | 20–25 nuts | 100 |
| Pistachio nuts | 12 nuts | 100 |
| Pine (pignolias) nuts | 1½ tablespoons | 100 |
| Walnuts | 4–8 nuts | 100 |

## SUGARS, SYRUPS, JAMS

| | | |
|---|---|---|
| Apple butter | 1 tablespoon | 50 |
| Brown sugar | 1 tablespoon | 50 |
| Cane sugar | 1 tablespoon | 50 |
| Confectioners' sugar | 1 teaspoon | 25 |
| Cube sugar | 1 cube | 20 |
| Honeycomb | 1 tablespoon | 75 |
| Jams (all flavors) | 1 tablespoon | 50 |
| Jellies (all flavors) | 1 tablespoon | 50 |
| Maple sugar | 1-ounce piece | 100 |
| Maple syrup | 1 tablespoon | 66–100 |
| Marmalade (orange) | 1 tablespoon | 50 |
| Molasses | 1 tablespoon | 50 |
| Powdered sugar | 1 tablespoon | 75 |

## SANDWICHES
### (INCLUDES TWO SLICES BREAD, NO SPREAD)

| | | |
|---|---|---|
| Bacon and lettuce | 3 slices bacon | 275 |
| Bacon and tomato | 3 slices bacon | 300 |
| Cheese (all kinds) | 2 thin slices | 300 |
| Chicken (white meat) | 3 thin slices | 275 |
| Chicken liver | 2 pieces, sliced | 325 |
| Egg salad | 1 medium egg | 300 |
| Eggs (sliced) | 1 medium egg | 275 |
| Frankfurter | 1 medium | 300 |
| Ham | 2 thin slices | 400 |
| Ham and cheese | 2 thin slices | 450 |
| Hamburger | medium patty | 400 |
| Liverwurst | 2 medium slices | 450 |

| FOOD | APPROXIMATE MEASURE | CALORIES |
|---|---|---|
| Peanut butter | 2 tablespoons | 350 |
| Salami | 2 thin slices | 275 |
| Tuna | 3 tablespoons | 300 |
| Turkey | 2 thin slices | 275 |

## HORS D'OEUVRES (INCLUDES COCKTAIL SAUCE)

| | | |
|---|---|---|
| Caviar | 1 tablespoon | 100 |
| Clams (bluepoint) | 6 medium (raw) | 75–100 |
| Clams (cherrystone) | 6 medium (raw) | 75–100 |
| Crab meat | ½ cup | 100 |
| Fruit cocktail | ½ cup | 75–80 |
| Gefuelte fish | ⅖ cup | 50 |
| Herring | 1 piece, 2-inch square | 100 |
| Lobster | ½ cup | 100 |
| Oysters | 6 medium (raw) | 75–100 |
| Shrimp | 6 medium (raw) | 75–100 |

## BEVERAGES—NONALCOHOLIC

| | | |
|---|---|---|
| Carbonated soda (sweet) | 8-ounce glass | 100 |
| Carbonated water | 8-ounce glass | 10 |
| Chocolate ice-cream soda | 10-ounce glass | 255 |
| Chocolate milk | 6-ounce glass | 208 |
| Chocolate milk (half milk) | 6-ounce glass | 146 |
| Chocolate milk shake | 8-ounce glass | 400–421 |
| Chocolate malted milk | 8-ounce glass | 400 |
| Cider | 8-ounce glass | 124–150 |
| Cocoa (all milk) | 6-ounce glass | 174–200 |
| Cocoa (half milk) | 6-ounce glass | 112 |
| Coffee (no sugar or cream) | 1 cup | None |
| Cola | 8-ounce glass | 106–150 |
| Eggnog | 8-ounce glass | 350–391 |
| Fruit punch (sweetened) | 8-ounce glass | 200 |
| Ginger ale | 8-ounce glass | 80–150 |
| Lemonade | 8-ounce glass | 104–150 |
| Malted milk (with ice cream) | 8-ounce glass | 600 |
| Orangeade | 8-ounce glass | 150 |
| Ovaltine (with skim milk) | 8-ounce glass | 200 |
| Postum (no sugar or cream) | 1 cup | 10–34 |
| Root beer | 8-ounce glass | 106–150 |
| Sarsaparilla | 8-ounce glass | 106–150 |
| Tea (no cream or sugar) | 1 cup | None |
| Tea (with one slice lemon) | 1 cup | 10 |
| Vanilla ice-cream soda | 10-ounce glass | 260 |
| Milk (fresh, whole) | 8-ounce glass | 166–168 |
| Milk (fresh, skimmed) | 8-ounce glass | 86–87 |

(Add 25 calories for each tablespoon of cream used, 20 calories for each teaspoon of sugar added to coffee or tea. Saccharine is a beverage sweetener that has no caloric value.)

# BEER, WINES, AND SPIRITS

| FOOD | APPROXIMATE MEASURE | CALORIES |
|---|---|---|
| Ale | 8-ounce glass | 100–150 |
| Beer (bock) | 8-ounce glass | 175 |
| Beer (lager) | 8-ounce glass | 114–125 |
| Brandy | Brandy glass | 75 |

## CORDIALS

| | | |
|---|---|---|
| Anisette | Cordial glass | 75–80 |
| Benedictine | Cordial glass | 70–85 |
| Creme de cacao | Cordial glass | 68–100 |
| Creme de menthe | Cordial glass | 68–100 |
| Curaçao | Cordial glass | 55 |

## COCKTAILS

| | | |
|---|---|---|
| Alexander | cocktail glass | 250 |
| Daiquiri | cocktail glass | 124–145 |
| Eggnog | 4-ounce cup | 338 |
| Manhattan | cocktail glass | 150–167 |
| Martini | cocktail glass | 100–143 |
| Mint julep | 8-ounce glass | 200–217 |
| Old-fashioned | 4-ounce glass | 145–183 |
| Planter's punch | punch glass | 177 |
| Tom and Jerry | mug | 250 |

## WHISKIES

| | | |
|---|---|---|
| Applejack | 1-ounce jigger | 100 |
| Bourbon | 1-ounce jigger | 100 |
| Gin | 1-ounce jigger | 100–107 |
| Irish | 1-ounce jigger | 100 |
| Rum | 1-ounce jigger | 100 |
| Rye | 1-ounce jigger | 100 |
| Scotch | 1-ounce jigger | 85 |

## WINES

| | | |
|---|---|---|
| Champagne | 6-ounce glass | 150 |
| Claret | 3-ounce glass | 85 |
| Muscatel | 3-ounce glass | 85 |
| Port | 3-ounce glass | 160 |
| Sauterne | 3-ounce glass | 160 |
| Sherry | 3-ounce glass | 85 |
| Sour | 3-ounce glass | 85 |
| Sweet | 3-ounce glass | 108 |
| Vermouth (dry) | 3-ounce glass | 108 |
| Vermouth (sweet) | 3-ounce glass | 170 |

# SAVE TIME, WORK, MONEY WITH YOUR FREEZER

### 113 WAYS TO MAKE THE MOST OF THIS MODERN FROZEN-FOOD STORAGE CONVENIENCE

### WHAT SIZE? WHAT SHAPE?

*Look for combinations,* with the freezer at the bottom if your refrigerator door is opened and closed much more often than that of the freezing compartment. Why bend over any oftener than you must?

*Tall and upright, or wide and deep?* You have a choice of two styles of plug-in home freezers: upright and chest-type. Either is sized anywhere from a minimum of about seven to 20 cubic feet maximum for most uprights, sizes going larger in chest-types.

*If you're short of floor space,* you'll probably want an upright freezer. And since it's tall, it takes but little wall as well as floor space.

*Make sure your flooring is strong enough* to hold the weight of an upright freezer, though, since much weight in a filled upright freezer is concentrated in one relatively small floor area.

*The top of a chest-type freezer,* if you locate the appliance in kitchen or utility room, provides counter space that is sometimes as needed and welcome as the addition of the convenient freezer itself.

*A giant home freezer* can be built right into your home. It's actually a refrigerated room like the one your butcher disappears into that's filled with his meat supplies.

*Freezer management* will be more successfully experienced if you proceed gradually. Don't, for instance, fill the freezer with the first products of the season. As the year passes, you'll want to add many things.

*Freeze foods as fast as possible.* To do this make sure they are in contact with the sides of the freezer chest or on the permanently refrigerated shelves of your upright.

*Organizing your freezer,* with special sections for meat, fruit, vegetables, breads, and other food specialties simplifies finding items quickly when you are planning a freezer meal. You might also like to have separate storage sections for beef, lamb, poultry, etc.

*Some combined meals,* sometimes called TV dinners, can be stored together for unexpected dinner guests, school lunches, or special diets.

*Use your freezer* for day-to-day meals, so frozen foods are in prime condition when they become part of your menus. Refer to the following guide for length of storage time for various foods, since some foods do not keep well frozen as long as others do.

*You'll want to keep an inventory* to help you remember quantities of various foods and length of time they've been in your freezer. Keep the record accurately so you'll know when to replenish supplies as well as when to use up foods that have reached their time limit in the frozen state.

*Take your pick of record keepers.* An inventory list on a blackboard near the freezer, with a magnetized pencil that sticks to the actual board; a record book, a card file, a calendar—these are all good ways to know all the time just what you have in your freezer.

## *Recommended Storage Period at Zero°F.

### FRUITS

Apples (sliced), 12 months
Apricots (when packed with ascorbic acid), 12 months
Blackberries (with sugar or syrup), 12 months
Boysenberries (with sugar or syrup), 12 months
Cherries (sour), 12 months
Cranberries, 12 months
Fruit juices (except citrus), eight to 12 months
Fruits and juices, citrus (in glass jars, with ascorbic acid),
    four to six months
Grapes, eight to 12 months
Huckleberries, 12 months
Loganberries (with sugar or syrup), 12 months
Melon balls, six to eight months
Peaches (when packed with ascorbic acid), 12 months
Pineapple, 12 months
Plums (when packed with ascorbic acid), 12 months
Raspberries (with sugar or syrup), 12 months
Rhubarb, 12 months
Strawberries (with sugar or syrup), 12 months

### VEGETABLES

Asparagus, six to eight months
Beans (bush), eight to 12 months
Beans (lima), 12 months
Beans (pole), eight to 12 months
Beans, soy (green), eight to 12 months
Beets, 12 months
Broccoli, 12 months
Brussels sprouts, eight to 12 months
Carrots, 12 months
Cauliflower, 12 months
Corn on the cob, eight to 12 months
Eggplant, eight to 12 months
Kohlrabi, eight to 12 months

* New techniques develop constantly. If you question storage time
listed above, consult your State College Extension Service for latest
home freezing information.

Okra, 12 months
Parsnips, 12 months
Peas, 12 months
Peppers, eight to 12 months
Potatoes, sweet, 12 months
Pumpkin, 12 months
Rutabagas, 12 months
Spinach and other greens, 12 months
Squash (summer), eight to 12 months
Squash (winter), 12 months
Tomatoes (stewed), six to eight months
Turnips, 12 months
Vegetables, mixed, eight to 12 months

## MEAT, MEAT PRODUCTS, FISH

Bacon (not sliced), three to four months
Bacon (sliced), less than one month
Beef, eight to 12 months
Beef, ground, four to six months
Beef liver, hearts, kidneys, three to four months
Cream, heavy (50 per cent), three to four months
Fish, lean (bass, cod, perch, pike, sunfish, etc.), six to eight months
Fish, fat (catfish, herring, mackerel, whitefish, etc.), three to four months
Fish, some fatty (especially pink salmon), two to three months
Game birds, eight to 12 months
Geese, three to four months
Ham, three to four months
Lamb, eight to 12 months
Liver, beef or calf, three to four months
Oysters, four to six months

Pork, fresh, four to six months
Pork, ground (unsalted), three to four months
Poultry (except broilers), six to eight months
Poultry giblets (except liver), two to three months
Poultry liver, less than one month
Poultry (cut-up), four to six months
Poultry, broilers, four to six months
Rabbit, eight to 12 months
Sausage (seasoned, not smoked), less than one month
Sausage (smoked and seasoned), two to three months
Shrimp or shellfish, cooked, two to three months
Turkeys, six to eight months
Veal, six to eight months
Venison, eight to 12 months
Wieners, two to three months

## PREPARED FOOD

Bread, baked yeast, two to three months
Bread, baked quick, two to three months
Cake and cupcakes, baked (frosted), less than one month
Cake, baked fruit, eight to 12 months
Cake and cupcakes, baked (unfrosted), two to three months
Cheese, Cheddar, six to eight months (and processed)
Pie, baked and unbaked, two to three months
Foods, cooked leftover, less than one month
Foods, most cooked, two to three months
Rolls, baked yeast, two to three months
Sandwiches, less than one month
Cookies, eight to 12 months
Pies, chiffon, less than one month

## MISCELLANEOUS

Eggs (not in shell), eight to 12 months
Butter, creamery, six to eight months
Lard, six to eight months
Cream, 40 per cent, three to four months
Coconut, shredded, eight to 12 months
Milk, pasteurized, homogenized, two weeks or less
Nuts, eight to 12 months
Ice cream, two to four weeks

*Parsley* can be frozen for use in soups, stews, etc., and minced while still frozen and crisp.

*Bean coffee,* if you grind your own and buy it in quantity, keeps very well in your freezer, better than on the pantry shelf.

*Shaved and crushed ice* are handy to have stored in moisture-vaporproof bags, as are a supply of extra ice cubes.

*Coffee and iced tea* can be frozen in ice-cube trays, the cubes tucked into freezer bags, and you'll have a supply on hand at a minute's notice.

*Cigars or cigarettes* keep well when frozen, stored in original box and dropped into freezer bags. Remove small amounts as needed or desired.

*Furs,* if stored at home, can be wrapped in moisture-vaporproof material and placed in the freezer for two days. This will kill any moth larvae. Remove and store in cool, dry place, leaving the wrapping material on during storage.

# THE KITCHEN HINT PARADE

*Double-boiler food saver.* A jar lid, placed in the bottom of the double boiler, will rattle when the water gets too low, and thus give you a dependable S.O.S.

*When frying fish or meat,* cover skillet with a colander. This allows steam to escape, permits food to brown well, and prevents grease from spattering.

*To keep whipping bowl from slipping,* set it on a folded damp cloth.

*Kitchen tools need oiling?* Apply a little glycerin with eye dropper. If any glycerin accidentally gets into food, don't worry. It's harmless.

*Clean out hard-to-remove sediment* that often clings to bottom of bottle or glass vase by filling vessel half full with warm soapsuds, then add a handful of carpet tacks. Shake vigorously and watch the sediment loosen.

*Corks can stick in bottles* containing sugary liquids (sweetened extracts, etc.). Prevent this by smoothing a bit of waxed paper or aluminum foil around cork before inserting it in opening.

*Save dishwashing time.* Use your china in rotation, so that there's never a group at the bottom of the pile that remains unused. Always take dishes from the bottom of the pile, and when they've been washed and wiped, return to the top spot. That way, none gathers dust.

*Deodorize inside of refrigerator* by washing it with soapy water containing a little baking soda.

*Another refrigerator deodorizer.* A lump of charcoal in your refrigerator soaks up fish, onion, and other strong odors. Prevents them from penetrating butter, cheese, and other sensitive foods.

*Goodbye to unwelcome cooking odors.* Neutralize them by boiling three teaspoonfuls of ground clove in two cups water for 15 minutes. Or heat some vinegar on range. Works like a charm.

*To locate a leak in a gas pipe,* brush pipe with thick suds. If hole is present, escaping gas will cause bubbles to form at the leaky spot.

*Rust rings caused by scouring-powder cans* sitting on shelves in the bathroom or kitchen can be prevented by covering bottom edges of the can with strips of scotch tape.

*To prevent egg white from spreading when poached,* add 1 teaspoon salt or a few drops of vinegar to each cup of water used for poaching.

*Save your large-size paper grocery bags.* They make excellent lining for garbage pail or wastebasket, make disposal of refuse easier, keep receptacle clean. Paper-bag line all your wastebaskets, for the same reason.

*Lick your postage problem.* A cut potato surface is just moist enough to use for stamps. Saves you the unpleasant chore of licking stamps and having the taste of glue on your tongue. Wonderful when you have lots of envelopes to send out, as at Christmastime.

*Brighten dulled aluminum pans* by boiling some apple parings in them.

*Stop frying-pan explosions.* A little salt sprinkled in the frying pan will keep fat or lard from spattering. Also makes range cleaning easier.

*Line the bottom of waste cans* with circles of aluminum foil. The foil will prevent the can from rusting and will keep it like new.

*Use foil to reheat rolls,* coffee cakes, and buns, in a 350°F. oven, and they'll have a fresh-baked flavor that makes them doubly delicious.

*Salt is usually hard to pour* in damp or muggy weather. Try this trick: Wrap a small piece of aluminum foil tightly around the top of the shaker. Moisture-vaporproof, the aluminum foil keeps dampness out of the salt, allows the salt to pour freely. Replace the "lid" immediately after using the shaker.

*For bottles that can't be recorked,* with their own stoppers, keep a supply of corks on hand and build them up to fit by wrapping aluminum foil around them.

*If you haven't a low flower bowl,* but still want a really special Christmas-table decoration, take one of your cake pans and cover it completely with aluminum foil. Mold the foil tightly to the pan and make a deep ruffle of foil to attach to the edge of the pan. Spread chicken wire or lay a frog in the center of the pan and arrange your evergreen sprigs and pine cones.

### THE LITTLE THINGS THAT MAKE A BIG DIFFERENCE

*Candlelight can be beautiful,* unless the romantic touch starts to drip. Avoid messy candles by putting them in refrigerator for a few hours before using.

*Attractive hangers for pot-holder hooks.* Use plastic shower hooks. They're rustproof, colorful, and allow pot holders to be hung easily from screw-hook or nail.

*Probation corner for new recipes.* Paste a large, strong envelope in the back of your favorite cookbook. Put in untried or clipped recipes, until you have time to test them and decide whether you want them in your permanent recipe file.

*Refrigerator stunt with muffin tin.* Use compartments of tin for storing partially used jars of baby food.

*Heating baby food quickly.* You can heat different kinds at the same time, by using a two- or three-cup egg poacher. When food is warm, lift it from tray, and feed Baby directly from the cups.

# HOW TO BE WELL DRESSED ON A BUDGET

*Save without skimping.* Watch for midseason and end-of-season sales. Make sure that sales are genuine, that reductions are genuine. Rely on the large department stores and on smaller stores with whose regular prices you are familiar.

*Multiply a small wardrobe.* Have garments in colors that harmonize with one another and are interchangeable. Variety of removable dickies and scarfs will do wonders. Plan your wardrobe so you can mix-match various sweaters, skirts, jackets, etc.

*When buying washables,* dresses and blouses that save time and money formerly spent on trips to the dry cleaner, stay away from garments with fussy details, because these often turn into real pressing problems.

*Short girls look taller* in straight or princess-style coats, simply tailored, or feminine dresses with straight or slightly flared skirts. Stick to smooth fabrics or solid colors, small prints. Stay away from large sleeves, large purses, large-brim hats.

*If you're tall,* make the most of it. Enjoy wearing large hats and purses, wide sleeves and belts, full skirts. Wear gay plaid jacket with solid-color skirt, flare-back coats, and the striking blouses and skirts in patterned fabrics.

*Tight fits didn't "shrink at the cleaner's,"* usually. If you are plump, get the size that gives you breathing space when you buy wools, sweaters, or any loose weaves like crepe, especially acetate crepe. Flat and close weaves are recommended, since they shrink hardly at all when dry-cleaned.

*Dress thin figure* smartly in bulky materials, plaids,

checks, feminine frills, and dirndl skirts. Shun severely tailored, straight-line clothes.

*For brownettes:* Greens, blues, blue-greens, add more color. Tan, red, orange will camouflage freckles. Most pastels and dusty colors are more flattering than white.

*For brunettes:* Vivid shades and stark whites do wonders. Bright, clear, warm tones are fine for those with high coloring. Cool green and blue-green tones add more color to the pale-skinned.

*For blondes:* Because hair tones vary widely, experiment until you find your best colors. Generally, blue, blue-purple, and blue-green are fine. Navy blue and dark shades are better than gray and beige. Greens heighten natural color, rosy tones make it paler. Dark tones are more flattering than pastels.

*For redheads:* Deep or dark colors highlight hair, browns and orange-tans tone it down. White, pale blue, pearly gray, and soft, dusty pastels are most becoming. Light redheads should wear deep blue and blue-purple. Note about freckles: Less obvious when wearing tan or orange-brown than with blue or green outfit.

## HOW TO COPE WITH SHINE, LINT, HAIRLINES

*Remove shine from wool clothes.* Sponge garment with solution of one teaspoon ammonia to a quart of water. Press on wrong side.

*Remove shine from serge,* as well as worsted gabardines, flannels, and worsted wools in general, by dampening a sponge or cloth slightly and sponging the shiny parts quite thoroughly. While fabric is damp, go over it, gently, with fine steel wool. With this, stroke the fabric, covering about six inches of the suit with each stroke.

*Remove lint from small area.* Wrap adhesive or scotch tape around your finger, sticky side out, then use as a pick-up. For larger area, wrap tape around a rolled-up magazine, sticky side out, and roll off the lint.

*Hairlines are danger lines* on men's and women's clothes. Once that oil mark hardens in the fabric, it may prove impossible to remove completely. So once weekly, clean coat-collar hairlines with cleaning fluid and brush briskly afterward.

### A STITCH IN TIME

*Save garment with clever embroidery trick.* Cover a small hole in a blouse or dress with a pretty bit of colorful embroidery design, and actually profit by an accident to the fabric, by giving the garment a new look. Cover frayed cuffs with closely sewn blanket stitch and add matching touch at neckline.

*Have you a growing daughter?* Let out the hems of her dresses at the end of the season, before they're cleaned or laundered and stored. When she's ready to wear them again, and needs dresses a little longer, a new hem can be made without any telltale mark to show the position of last year's hemline.

*Friction foiler.* Elbows of long-sleeve woolen dresses usually are the first to show wear. Reinforce these weak spots by sewing an oblong piece of lightweight fabric of the same color inside the elbow.

*When a zipper jams.* You'll probably find that paper or

thread particles are interfering with its free play. These must be removed patiently. Wherever an end of thread or fabric protrudes, pull it out gently. If the slider still jams, move it back and forth until you loosen the impediment. Always hold the slider by the tab. Never push, pull, or poke.

*Zippers always work smoothly,* when teeth are rubbed occasionally with a bit of wax.

*Line the pockets of trousers* with chamois to protect the pockets from tears made by nails, bolts, and small tools carried around by some men and boys.

*"To each his own."* Where there are several children wearing jeans of about the same size, it is sometimes difficult to tell which pair belongs to whom. With an indelible pencil, mark their names or initials on the inside white band or pockets.

### GETTING THE HANG OF IT

*The wrong way is right.* Put garments on hangers wrong-side out. Keeps them clean longer.

*Here's a trick up your nonexistent sleeve.* To prevent sleeveless garments from slipping off wire hangers, bend up both ends of the hanger.

*Wire hangers won't rust-stain clothes,* if you wind cellulose tape around them.

*Do wire hangers cave in* under weight of heavy garments? Double their strength by binding two hangers together with cellulose or adhesive tape.

*To prevent wooden hangers from snagging fabric,* give them a coat of clear shellac. Allow to dry well. Wood won't chip or sliver, if protected this way.

*Number the shirts.* Shirts should be rotated so that each gets equal wear. Why not number each shirt inside the neckband, to help keep track?

*Fadeout on fading.* Clothes of aquamarine or some shades of blue, purple, and gray tend to fade. They'll stay their true color longer if you store them between wearings in a black cloth bag or in black wrapping paper.

### HOW TO STARVE MOTHS

*Your mothproofing money's worth.* Moth preventives should be hung as high as possible in the clothes closet, because the fumes filter downward. Otherwise you get only partial protection.

*Moths love woolens.* Woolens don't love moths. One sure way to keep them apart in summertime is to store unused sweaters and other woolens in large jars stuffed with moth balls, the lid turned down.

*Moths love grease spots too.* That's why articles ready for storing should be dry-cleaned or laundered first.

*Moth balls on a hanger.* Drill two or three small holes near top of wooden-hanger beam. Press moth ball into hole, and fix in place with strips of tape, so they won't fall out as they grow smaller. Pierce the tape with pinholes.

### STOCKING SAVERS

*Hosiery glamour lasts longer* if you buy your dressy sheers half a size longer than usual. You avoid strain at the toes, where runs often start.

*Dyeing gives new life.* Stockings of different shades can be matched for plenty of extra wear by dyeing them. Get a package of color remover and a package of dye. Follow instructions on the packages.

*Easy to pair.* Sew a different colored thread at the top of each pair of stockings. This makes it easy to identify and pair them after washing.

*Saves hosiery.* If the leather on the inside of the heel of your shoe wears through, cover the hole with a piece of very flatly fitting adhesive tape. You'll stop wearing holes in your hosiery.

*Rainy-weather protection for sheer hose.* Place strips of adhesive tape around inside of galoshes at top. Keeps them from leaving rings on your stockings.

# LAUNDRY-CLEANING-IRONING

EXPERTS GIVE YOU THEIR LABORATORY-TESTED
DIRECTIONS

*In cleaning, follow the fabric's own preference.* The following chart tells you whether washing or dry-cleaning is the natural requirement of a given material, also the best ironing procedure for each of the basic fabrics:

| FABRIC | CLEANING METHOD | IRONING METHOD |
|---|---|---|
| Cotton | Wash. Check label for instructions on texture types. | Minimum pressing for embossed surfaces. While still damp, press on wrong side with hot iron. |
| Linen | Wash. Household bleach is all right for white table linens, bedclothes. | Iron on wrong side, while damp. Go easy on crease-resistant linens. |
| Silk | Outer garments usually dry-cleaned. Wash only if recommended by instructions. Don't hang in sun to dry. | On wrong side, with moderate iron. |
| Wool | Outer garments, usually dry-cleaned. Sweaters, etc., should be washed carefully in lukewarm water, mild suds. Never soak or rub. Dry flat. Air frequently; brush after wearing. Clean before storing. | Steam-press, when necessary. Use cloth between articles and iron. |
| Rayon | Consult label to determine washability. Mild suds, warm (not hot) water. Rinse with extra care. Brush. Air often to avoid mildew. | Moderate iron on wrong side. |

| FABRIC | CLEANING METHOD | IRONING METHOD |
|---|---|---|
| Acetate | Launder at low temperature. To avoid permanent wrinkles, don't wring. | Use low-heat iron. |
| Nylon | Generally washable, but may be dry-cleaned. White garments will retain whiteness if washed often. Special bleaches available if they begin to "gray." Mild soaps or detergents recommended. | Requires little pressing. Use moderate iron. |
| Dacron | Used in blends and washable, if other fibers in mixture are. Medium-hot water. Check label. | Depends on other fibers in blend. Consult label. |
| Orlon | Wash in moderate-to-hot water. Drip-dry if pleated. | Low temperature, requires very little pressing. |
| Arnel or Acrilan | Wash in moderate-to-hot water. Drip-dry if pleated. | Low temperature, requires very little pressing. |

*Just how warm* should the correct water temperature be for the various basic fabrics? Here's the answer:

| FABRIC | WATER TEMPERATURE | OR IN OTHER WORDS: |
|---|---|---|
| White cottons and linens (machine washing) | 140°F., and up. | Much too hot for hands. |
| White cottons and linens (hand washing) | 120°F. | As hot as hand can bear. |
| Fast-color cottons, linens, nylons | 110°F. | Warm or comfortable for hands. |
| Rayons | 100–110°F. | Lukewarm to warm. |
| Silks and woolens | 95–100°F. | Lukewarm. Feels neither hot nor cold to wrist or elbow. |

*Solve your hard-water problem* by consulting your city water department. Find out degree of water hardness in your area and ask what chemical compound will most effectively soften the water in your locality. You may be advised, for very hard water, to have a water softener installed in your home.

*For best laundering results,* sort clothes by grouping thus:

1. White cottons and linens with fast-color pastel cottons.
2. Dark, fast-color cottons and linens.
3. Fabrics requiring special care (wools, silks, rayons, nylons, etc.). Do the less-soiled articles first, follow with the more heavily soiled pieces.

*When sorting clothes,* before they go into washer, empty the pockets, examine for spots, stains, torn areas. Rips should be mended before washing, to prevent more tearing. Take off all removable trims and shoulder pads.

*Remove stains* before laundering, because hot water and suds may set some stains so they can't be removed later.

*Take the time to close zippers,* so they won't catch on other articles and rip them.

### TIME AND MONEY SAVERS

*Save time on laundry day.* Instead of measuring out soap, bleach, bluing, etc., every washday, put up proper mixtures in glass jars. You can prepare enough to last a few weeks.

*Fresh cake soap* will last longer if it is allowed to age a few weeks before using. Soap contains moisture, and should be unwrapped during aging, so moisture can evaporate.

*Soap thrift.* Save leftover slivers of soap in a jar. When half filled, add boiling water, to make a jelly. It will come in handy for lots of pretreating and light laundering.

*Too much thrift doesn't pay.* Don't use badly soiled wash water at any time. Such saving of water and cleanser is poor economy, because articles washed in soiled water never look, or are, really clean.

*Overwashed clothes may come out soiled.* Prolonged agitation of your washing machine often drives dirt back into fabrics. For lightly soiled pieces, five minutes is usually enough. Never allow washer to agitate for longer than 15 minutes, even for heavily soiled articles.

*To soak or not to soak.* Twenty minutes is plenty for cottons. Precaution: Never soak rayons (swells fibers and traps dirt particles), or color pieces (colors may run).

## STARCHING TIPS AND TRICKS

*Laundry starch* protects cotton and linen clothing and household linens from soiling. It restores the original finish to many fabrics, so that they don't have to be washed so often, thus saving wear and tear.

*When preparing laundry starch,* you'll avoid formation of skin over it if you cover the bowl with a piece of cloth, stretched tight, as soon as the starch is made.

*Starched garments dried in an automatic dryer* should be done separately. Otherwise, some starch may come off on unstarched fabrics. Also, starch a little heavier than you would for line drying because some starch tumbles off as garments are dryer-dried. Remember too, that you'll want to wipe off the dryer cylinder after using it for starched garments, so that no starch deposits on succeeding dryer loads.

*Starched clothes iron best,* if allowed to dry thoroughly before sprinkling.

*Remember to starch curtains* of very sheer material lightly before stretching.

## RIGHT DRYING

*Unroll garments immediately* after towel drying. Leaving them rolled up for any length of time may cause rot, mildew, and other damage.

*Streaks will be avoided* and moisture will evaporate evenly, if you'll dry nylon stockings on damp towels.

*A washed sweater will not stretch* if you rinse it in a colander and squeeze out the excess water gently.

*If you haven't a form* on which to stretch washed gloves,

use an old curling iron. It will do the job of stretching the fingers before they are thoroughly dry.

*To make a drying rack* for small articles, sew spring paper clips to tape on an ordinary clothes hanger.

*If you use the neighborhood launderette,* take a plastic pillow case to tote home your sprinkled clothes. They'll stay nicely damp until you get ready to iron them.

### IRONING OUT YOUR DIFFICULTIES

*Sprinkling cuts ironing time,* if not overdone. If clothes are too wet, ironing becomes more difficult, takes longer.

*A real ironing short cut* is yours if you hang on one line all clothes to be ironed. When they're dry, sprinkle with fine-spray garden hose, all at once. Then roll up each piece as you remove it from the line.

*Sprinkling small, flat pieces* takes less time if all pieces of similar size are shaken out and placed in a pile. Sprinkle about every third piece, roll together, smoothing fabric as you go. Roll tightly.

*Lukewarm water* is better for sprinkling than cold, penetrates much faster, more evenly.

*Large and long pieces,* like tablecloths and sheets, have a tendency to dry up quickly during ironing. To avoid this, pin a Turkish towel to the ironing board, to act as an envelope. Place the long item in the Turkish-towel envelope and pull out as you iron.

*Steam iron* keeps accessories and high-fashion garments looking lovely longer. Velvet, velveteen, corduroy, and suede, all high in the fashion picture, are pile fabrics. Dresses, coats, hats, bags, and even shoes of these materials will keep their attractive finish longer with steam treatment. Hold steam iron just above fabric and allow steam to penetrate and raise the nap.

*Collar shiny?* Sponge it first with vinegar, then press on the wrong side. No more shine.

*Your dark cottons* won't pick up lint from ironing board, if you use this trick: Before starting to iron, go over the cover with a damp cloth or sponge, or a wide piece of cellophane tape, or some adhesive tape wound around your hand, sticky side out.

*When ironing double thicknesses*, such as collars, cuffs, pockets, hems, iron first on the wrong side, then on the right side.

*To prevent wrinkling clothes* while ironing, do the small parts first, in this order: Trimmings, collar, sleeves, back bodice, front bodice. Skirt part of dress should be the last.

# SPOTS AND STAINS

## AND HOW TO REMOVE THEM FROM WASHABLES AND NONWASHABLES

### THE A-B-C OF TERMS USED IN DIRECTIONS FOR STAIN REMOVAL

*Bleeding.* Loss of dye. If fabric is not colorfast, the dye may be loosened from the fabric under certain conditions (as when soaked in water). The color then is said to "bleed."

*Flushing out.* Removing stain by working it free from fabric by brushing, rinsing, etc.

*Sizing.* A stiffening agent used in fabrics. Sometimes fabric itself is weighted with resinous or other substances. Sometimes it comes in separate stiffening fabrics, like buckram, employed to give extra firmness to collars, facing, belts, etc.

*Spotting.* The actual process of removing spots and stains. Methods for spotting include:

*Lubrication.* Using cleansers with oil bases.

*Solvent action.* Use of so-called "wet" and "dry" solutions for dissolving stains.

*Mechanical action.* Scraping, rubbing, brushing, etc.

*Wet cleaning and dry cleaning.* Terms to indicate whether a specific stain responds to treatment by so-called "wet" or "dry" cleansing agents. Wet cleaners are liquids, the most important being water. Dry ones contain no actual moisture, even when liquid in form.

*Acids* (*wet-clean*). First rinse with cold water. If any solid substance is imbedded in stain, you may have to flush it out with a fairly concentrated solution of neutral detergent. If acid is strong mineral type (like hydrochloric or sulfuric battery acid), follow cold water treatment with application of ammonia to completely neutralize it. Such strong acids will quickly damage cotton, rayon, etc. Wool is more resistant, but sufficient acid concentration can also damage it. Color changes caused by acid stain can usually be neutralized with household ammonia and water.

*Alcoholic beverages* (*wet-clean*). Rinse immediately from fabric with cold water, especially if fabric is cellulose acetate, because acetate yarns bleed profusely in alcohol and loss of color often results. Since alcohol is readily soluble in water, it will come out easily. If other food substances are present, remove with neutral detergent.

*Ammonia stains* (*wet-clean*). Ammonia may bleed dye or cause color change. Color changes can be corrected by applying white vinegar and water to affected area.

*Blood* (*wet-clean*). If fabric can withstand plain water, soak it first in a pan or bowl of cold water, or between two wet towels. Add about ½ teaspoon neutral detergent to soaking bath. When using towels, apply concentrated solution of detergent to the stain itself, this usually being enough to remove it. If stain still persists, apply small amount of household ammonia to area and rub between your fingers (unless fabric is acetate) or use back of comb to help break up stain. Flush from fabric as necessary. Hydrogen peroxide can also be effective, if fabric can stand such bleaching.

*Bluing (wet-clean)*. Soak stain in solution of water to which you've added ½ teaspoon of neutral detergent and about one ounce of household ammonia. Soak for about an hour if color of fabric permits, then launder. If any of the stain remains, next step is bleaching. For rayon, cotton, or acetate, use weak solution of chlorine bleach. For silk or wool, use hydrogen peroxide.

*Candy (wet-clean)*. Since mostly sugar, candy stains are usually easy to remove by sponging out with plain water. In more stubborn cases, a neutral detergent in the water will help.

*Carrot juice (wet-clean)*. In washables, this stain usually comes out in laundering. If not, treat stained area with solution of water and neutral detergent.

*Catsup (wet-clean)*. Remove as soon as possible, because age makes this one hard to budge. First flush as much of stain as possible in fairly concentrated solution of neutral detergent and water. Lubricate remaining portions of stain with glycerin, working it in with blunt edge of knife or back of comb. Then flush again with detergent-and-water solution.

*Coffee (wet-clean)*. Treat as soon as possible, because tannin compounds in coffee are impossible to remove once they're dried. If possible, soak stained area in bowl of warm water and neutral detergent solution. Watch to detect quickly if any bleeding of dye occurs. If it does, soak immediately in cold water and stop working on it. If no dye bleeds, soak in original solution, then flex between fingers (except taffeta or satin, etc.). If necessary, work some glycerin into stain and soak again. Avoid hot water and alkalies (like soap). On white cotton, rayon, or acetate, use bleaching solution of chlorine to remove remaining traces. Then wash, if fabric is dyefast. For wool and silk, bleach with milder agent like hydrogen peroxide (drugstore variety).

*Egg stains (wet-clean)*. Scrape any caked-on residue from fabric with dull edge of knife. Apply cold water and neutral detergent and allow to soak in such a solution for few minutes, depending on tendency of dye to bleed. Brush, or flex between fingers to loosen particles imbedded in fabric. If necessary, lubricate area with glycerin or neutral detergent (in heavily concentrated form). Then apply soap or neutral detergent to stain, plus ammonia. Tamp with brush or flex with fingers. Then flush area, wipe it dry, or launder garment.

*Fish slime (wet-clean)*. This is a concentrated albumen stain and can be very difficult to remove, impossible on certain resin-treated or sized fabrics. Soak stained area immediately in pan containing solution of water with some neutral detergent and about a spoonful of salt. Soak about ten minutes and flex slightly between fingers or tamp with brush. Rinse in plain cold water. Should stain remain, further home treatment is not advisable. Send to dry cleaner, identifying the stain.

*Fruits and fruit juices (wet-clean)*. Brown or tan stains resulting from fruit juice are due to sugar in the fruit. Often stains don't show at once, but the stain may set as fruit sugar dries and caramelizes (turning brown), the way sugar does under high heat. Once caramelized, such stains become difficult to treat, and practically impossible on wool. Flush stain as soon as possible in a solution of water and neutral detergent. Soaking may also help. If stain remains, try few drops of white vinegar, then flush again in detergent and water. Don't use high heat on the stain, since this speeds up caramelization and only sets the stain faster.

*Gelatin stains (wet-clean)*. Normally laundering will remove such stains, provided water is not over 100°F. Hot suds and rinses tend to set rather than remove stain.

*Glue or mucilage (wet-clean)*. Soak out stain in lukewarm water and neutral detergent, then apply some household ammonia and tamp with brush or flex between fingers. Rinse, then wipe area with dry cloth.

*Grass stains (wet-clean)*. Test fabric to see if it will withstand alcohol by applying some to hidden area (like the seam). If this is all right, use alcohol to remove green color, then lubricate area with concentrated detergent solution and flush both alcohol and detergent out of fabric with cold water. Next apply a few drops of household ammonia to stain and at the same time work in more detergent solution. Flush again with cold water and launder if possible. Otherwise, wipe area with dry cloth and let dry.

*Ink: Red, blue, black, etc. (wet-clean)*. Place towel or cheesecloth under stained area. Then apply concentrated solution of neutral detergent, working in with blunt-edged object. White or light-colored pieces of blotting paper can be used to absorb some of the dye from top of stain as ink starts to bleed. Repeat until bleeding stops. Then add a few drops of white vinegar to stain, along with more detergent. As bleeding begins again, repeat treatment with blotter and towel until bleeding stops. After this, apply household ammonia and detergent to remove remaining traces of dyestuff. Beyond this, bleaches will be necessary, but only if color-fastness and type of fabric fiber permit. Don't use milk on ink stain. Usually milk is harder to remove than ink and doesn't help stain removal. Sometimes wet-side inks can be removed best with a solution of water and neutral detergent.

*Iodine (wet-clean)*. Quickly remove with sodium thiosulphate crystals (usually called hypo crystals) that are available at drugstores. Place some crystals in piece of cheesecloth, moisten them, and pat stained area with wet crystals. Drop of ammonia tends to speed up action, but stain usually disappears quickly anyway. Rinse with cold water and wipe with dry cloth.

*Iron rust*. Use either commercial rust remover (hydrofluoric acid) or get oxalic-acid crystals at drugstore. Place a few in cheesecloth, moisten, and apply to stain. After stain is removed, be sure to rinse acid completely from fabric.

*Lead pencil (wet-clean)*. Work glycerin or heavy detergent solution into stains with blunt-edged object. Apply few drops of ammonia and gently work into stain. As stains dissolve, flush from fabric with warm water.

*Liquor stains, alcohol (wet-clean)*. Alcohol content can be particularly damaging to acetate fabrics because it bleeds their dyes so severely. The longer stain remains, the more the damage. Sponge area immediately with solution of water and neutral detergent. If fruit juices are also present, follow procedure given for their removal, after rinsing out the alcohol. It may be necessary to let your cleaner take over further spotting activity.

*Mercurochrome (wet-clean)*. Easy to flush out of acetates and nylons. Most difficult to remove from wool. Dyes in mercurochrome will bleed if alkali is used, so first apply some glycerin or concentrated solution of detergent and water. As stain bleeds, soak up as much as possible with blotting paper and have towel underneath to absorb the stain that is flushed from fabric. After bleeding stops with only a neutral detergent, add few drops of household ammonia. This will cause further bleeding. Continue working with detergent and ammonia until bleeding stops. Rinse with water to which small amount of white vinegar has been added. Then (on white fabrics only) bleach if necessary. Use chlorine bleach for cotton, acetate, rayon, or nylon; hydrogen peroxide for wool or silk.

*Mildew (wet-clean)*. If garment is washable, first launder in soap-and-ammonia solution. If color will withstand bleaching action of chlorine bleach, use that. Don't try to do job on wool or fancy fabrics. Play safe; give it to your dry cleaner.

*Milk (wet-clean)*. Sponge area with neutral detergent and water, then add few drops of ammonia to area and continue detergent solution. If necessary, tamp stain with brush or work back and forth across it with blunt-edged object. For old milk stains, it may be necessary to use an enzyme (like powdered pepsin), available at drugstores. Soak in solution of water and pepsin at least twenty minutes at temperature slightly above lukewarm. After soaking, repeat above procedure. Milk stains may be impossible to remove on some resin-treated fabrics.

*Mud (wet-clean)*. Allow to dry. Then dry-brush as much as possible from garment. Sponge remaining mud with warm solution of water and detergent. Launder, or flush out with plain water, and wipe down with dry cloth.

*Mustard* (*wet-clean*). On washables, apply glycerin. After working it into stain, flush with detergent and water. Do not use soap. If stain remains, better let dry cleaner try. Even he, however, may not be able to eliminate yellow stain caused by a chemical in the mustard.

*Nail polish* (*dry-clean*). Dissolves in acetone or amyl acetate. However, do not use acetone if fabric is rayon, vinyon, acetate, or nylon, since it damages them. Note: Do not use nail polish remover on above-mentioned fabrics since it, too, often contains acetone.

*Perfume* (*wet-clean*). Flush from fabric with solution of detergent and water as soon as possible, because alcohol in perfume will severely bleed some dyes, such as acetate. If fabric has no acetate, small amount of alcohol added to detergent solution will help. Test first for colorfastness to alcohol.

*Perspiration* (*wet-clean*). When fresh, perspiration is acid in nature. However, bacteria act upon it quickly, turning it alkaline. For fresh stains, flush area with detergent, water, and ammonia in solution. For old stains (by now turned alkaline), use a solution of water, detergent, and vinegar. Sometimes, color damages occur from either acids or alkalies. An acid or alkali will restore the color, depending on which agent originally caused the color change.

*Plastic stains* (*dry-clean*). Follow same directions as for nail polish.

*Scorch* (*wet-clean*). If fabric will withstand chlorine bleach (rayon, acetate, nylon, etc.) and if dye will also react favorably, bleach as you wash. If scorch is on wool, apply hydrogen peroxide by spray or with a cloth (in this case, use rubber gloves). Then place garment so that stained area faces the sun. Watch from time to time until stain is gone. If necessary, apply more hydrogen peroxide as it dries out. If dye begins to lighten, stop procedure, and rinse peroxide from fabric.

*Soot* (*wet-clean*). Especially tough to remove, if soot stain is wet. Soak garment or affected area in heavy solution of detergent and water to lubricate, penetrate, and flush away stain. Watch fabric colors carefully if long soaking is necessary. If severe color bleeding starts, rinse garment or spot the area with cold water. (Some salt in the water usually checks or prevents bleeding.) If bleeding takes place, don't continue; let cleaner take over. Bleaching is ineffective, because soot is primarily carbon.

*Sugar syrup* (*wet-clean*). Follow same directions as for candy.

*Tea* (*wet-clean*). Normal washing will usually suffice, unless stain has been present a long time. If stain is stubborn, use chlorine bleach on white cotton or linen; hydrogen peroxide on silk or wool (if color will withstand the bleach).

*Tobacco juice* (*wet-clean*). Lubricate with glycerin, then soak garment or stained area in solution of detergent and lukewarm water. On whites, bleaching may be necessary, chlorine bleach for cottons and synthetics, hydrogen peroxide for silk and wool. Tobacco's tannin content makes it a difficult stain to remove.

*Tomato juice* (*wet-clean*). Follow same directions as for catsup.

*Tooth paste* (*wet-clean*). If dry, most of it can be dry-brushed off. Otherwise, usually easy to flush off with either soap-and-water or detergent-and-water solution. Since some tooth pastes contain sodium perborate (a bleach) guard against allowing stain to damage fabric; remove quickly.

*Water spots on taffeta* (*wet-clean*). If fabric shows spots, it contains considerable sizing that creates a problem. No home method will work. Dry cleaner has certain facilities that usually solve the situation.

*Wine* (*wet-clean*). Work on this stain as soon as possible. Apply concentrated solution of neutral detergent and some glycerin, working it into area. Allow to remain a few minutes, then sponge with clear water, about hand-warm (never hot). Flex stain between fingers while rinsing. If some color of wine remains, apply few drops of ammonia with some detergent to the stain. This may turn it from blue to pink. White vinegar will turn it back to original blue. Such a condition means that a so-called indicator dye is present and there is little you can do unless fabric can withstand bleaching.

# YOUR SEWING KIT

MAKING YOUR OWN . . . EXPERTISMS FOR AMA-
TEURS . . . TAKING THE KINKS OUT OF THREAD-
AND-NEEDLE TIME

*Tip to beginners.* Start with a fabric that is easy to handle. Choose a solid-color material. The problem of matching designs at the seams is a tricky one. Also, choose a style with a minimum of detail work.

*Fabric must be preshrunk.* Unless you are sure that it is, take your material to your cleaner's and have it shrunk before working with it.

*Handle your material as little as possible* once work on it has begun. Keep it on the worktable. If you don't have a special cutting board, spread material on a clean rug or carpet.

*Keep pins on hand.* Take a plastic bracelet and glue on it a long piece of foam rubber about 2 inches wide. Or attach a large powder puff to your wrist with a rubber band. These clever devices will also prove practical in fittings.

*To cut materials smoothly,* keep left hand on pattern, cutting along right edge; use sharp, medium shears; take long, smooth strokes; never quite close the shears.

*Before you remove the pattern* make sure you have put in all the markings for darts, tucks, lengthwise and crosswise grains, and have basting lines run down center front and center back.

*It isn't enough to know what size you are.* You have to know your exact measurements before you buy a pattern, and especially before you undertake to cut your material.

*The four most important measurements* of the feminine figure are, as you well know: the bust, the difference between the bust and the chest, the waist, and the hips.

*Determine right-size pattern from your measurements.* Your chest and bust measurements determine the size of the pattern you need. For full or flared skirt (if the skirt is a separate), use your waist measurement. For a straight skirt, take your hip measurement.

*In taking measurements* wear those foundation garments and shoes that you plan to wear with the finished dress.

*No pinholes, please.* If you have a lot of hemming and don't want to use pins, paper clips or bobby pins will do.

*To lengthen skirts* when you have no matching material

to provide good facings, try bandage gauze. It's preshrunk and doesn't pucker when laundered.

*To sew plastic* place a piece of newspaper under the material to keep it from sticking to the sewing machine.

*To rip long seams* hold the material under the presser foot of your sewing machine, making the presser foot serve as a "third hand."

*To prevent puckering,* when stitching sheer and stiff fabric such as taffeta, place a one-inch-wide strip of paper under the seam line while stitching.

*When sewing seams on lace or sheer garments,* stitch each seam twice, the second stitching ¼ inch from the first. Then trim the seam close to this second stitching. No other finishing will be necessary.

### YOUR OWN SEWING CIRCLE

*Sewing-kit champ.* If you have a spare ping-pong paddle, drive nails into it to hold spools for sewing and fix one or two small corks on the handle to hold the thimbles.

*Easier basting.* One woman has found that as much as 16 inches of material can be basted without moving the fabric, if it is pinned down to a pillow during the basting or hemming. Pillow is held in the lap, leaving both hands free to work.

*Cut basting thread, not fabric,* when removing the thread. Best way: cut between the stitches and pull out in short lengths. You may risk large thread holes, even tear fabric threads in sheer material, if you try to pull out long basting threads.

*Save thread; save mess.* Rubber bands slipped over spools of thread keep the ends of the thread from unwinding and cluttering your sewing box.

*Make a thread holder.* Unwind twist of wire hanger. Open short end. Form wire into circle. Slip on spools. Retwist wire to close circle. Hang pincushion from it. Hang circle in your sewing corner. You can then unwind thread as needed without removing spool from hanger.

*Spools won't fly off spindles* if you clamp a spring-type clothespin on the spindle just before you start winding bobbin on your sewing machine.

*Avoid a whirlspool.* Keep your spool from unwinding too rapidly on your machine by placing a small rubber faucet washer on top of the spool. Serves as friction brake.

*A handy thread cutter* that costs you nothing can be improvised with an empty container of dental floss. Wind length of thread on a cut-down drinking straw and slip loose end through opening in the cover of the container.

*Loose ends.* A rubber sponge will quickly and neatly pick up the loose threads from a line of stitching that has been ripped out.

*Use up your odds and ends* of colored thread for basting, using a different color for each type of marking.

*Use darning cotton to make tailor-tack markings.* It won't slip out of the fabric as easily as sewing thread.

*Double, double, have no trouble.* Next time you sew with double thread, pull through to even length, then knot each end separately instead of both together. Thread will not snarl or break as when two ends are knotted jointly.

*Remove rust from sewing needle or pin* by pressing it, tip first, into a piece of soap. Soap removes the rust, sterilizes needle.

*Sewing stiff fabrics* becomes easier if you occasionally stick your needle into a bar of soap. The soap lubricates the needle and makes the going smoother.

*If nylon fabrics pucker* along stitching lines, try using a sharp, new, finer machine needle and pasting a piece of heavy brown paper over the plate of the machine. This will reduce the size of the hole for the needle and prevent the fabric from being drawn down too far.

*To sharpen machine needles,* stitch a few inches through sandpaper.

*To sharpen scissors.* Cut through fine sandpaper several times.

*When ripping machine stitching,* a good pair of tweezers is a boon. Thread will pull out easier, make work much faster and less tedious.

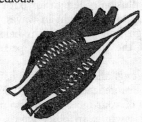

*Don't get stuck.* Just before taking up that hand sewing, try coating your finger tips with several layers of colorless nail polish as protection against needle cuts.

# YOUR BEAUTY SALON AT HOME

"SECRETS OF THE STARS" FROM JOHN ROBERT POWERS, MAX FACTOR, AND OTHER AUTHORITIES ON BEAUTY

## YOUR CROWNING GLORY

*"Can't do a thing with your hair?"* Try adding this simple ritual to your daily beauty program: Bend over and brush your scalp and hair from back to front until your scalp tingles. Then massage scalp with finger tips and see how easy to manage your hair becomes.

*Home treatment for dandruff.* Apply hot olive oil several hours before shampooing. Shampoo scalp thoroughly with tincture of green soap, which you can buy at any drugstore.

*If your face is round,* do not cut your hair so short that it fails to add the illusion of length to your face. You'll need enough hair on top to add height in waves, curls, etc. Also, you'll need enough hair to fall down below the lobes of your ears so that the illusion of the perfect oval face is created.

*If your face is long,* allow for enough hair to curl or dip over the side of your forehead, and enough on the side to add width to the sides of your face. You'll also need hair falling down below your jawline. In other words, your long face needs complete framing to create the wanted oval contour.

*If your face is a triangle,* a narrow forehead and wide jaws, your hair must never be cut so short that it causes the

jaws to stand out. They should be completely framed by a soft coiffure that falls below them. Furthermore, the narrow forehead should be widened by waves or curls to accentuate the oval illusion.

*If your face is an inverted triangle,* a wide forehead and narrow chin, your hair should never be cut so short that a pointed chin is left alone. Your hair should be cut and curled so that it is long enough to give width to the chinline, and so that dips and curls may cover part of the forehead to give balance to the contour.

*If your face is squarish,* wide forehead and wide jaws, be sure to leave your hair long enough to soften its contour into the perfect oval. Never crop your hair so short that jaws and forehead are left standing alone.

*If your face is a perfect oval,* you are a very lucky person indeed. Show this beauty by wearing the most simple styles possible. Your face type will look lovely with short hair or long. However, avoid extreme styles, for these can distort even a perfect face and lessen its natural glamour.

### "STARS GET IN YOUR EYES"

*To match the stars in your eyes,* apply mascara after making up the rest of your face completely. Brush off the excess and let it "set" for a few minutes. Then curl your lashes and add a little more mascara to the tips of your lashes. It's this last "tipping" that does most to give the alluring illusion of length.

*Close-set eyes?* To give the illusion of extra width and depth, apply your eye shadow on the upper lid, starting at the center of the eyelid and blending to the outer corner of each eye.

*Scarecrow for crow's feet.* Laugh wrinkles in the corner of your eyes come, not from age, but from relative skin dryness. So don't neglect daily, or nightly, lubrication with a good eye cream. Don't massage that delicate skin area. Pat cream lightly around outside corners of eyes, under eyes, and on eyelids.

*Detract attention from circles under your eyes* by adding blue eye shadow on and around your lids, discreetly blending the shade.

*Clear-eyed beauty.* The best eye care is, of course, lots of sleep, and avoidance of overstraining through reading, sewing, movies, or TV. If your eyes get tired easily, bathe occasionally with soothing eye lotion, and check with your eye doctor as to whether you need glasses.

*Use hot water* for the application of eyelash makeup. The warmth of the water seems to cause the makeup to go on more smoothly and lastingly than when cold water is used.

*To make the nose appear narrower,* apply a drop of dark blue, brown, or gray eye shadow alongside before applying powder. Make sure that you blend the eye shadow lightly to avoid spotty look.

### TRICKS WITH LIPSTICK

*Lipstick trick.* Use a colorfast lipstick, applied with a brush so that the lipline stays better put. Then blot, reapply, and blot again. Don't cheat on the time it takes lipstick color to set. It takes two full minutes for the first application.

*Lip contour.* Strive for smooth outlines, straightening and blending with one firm stroke of forefinger wrapped in cleansing tissue. You may stay a little inside the outline of a mouth you feel too full, or may go just slightly beyond the outline of thin lips, though not too much. Above all, don't try to change the shape too much. It will always show, will only look unnatural.

*All professional makeup artists* use lipstick brush to apply lipstick, and the actresses on whom they apply this beauty requisite soon learn how to use the brush themselves so that their lips look perfectly beautiful all the time.

*You can mend a broken lipstick.* All you have to do is heat the broken ends over a gas, match, or cigarette lighter flame, until they melt enough to adhere when you press them together. Then, don't use the lipstick until the ends have had enough time to get together and cool.

*Your teeth are important.* Your teeth may not be perfect and even, but your mouth can still be attractive if your teeth are sparkling. Regular dental care is the best assurance for keeping teeth in good condition. The most carefully applied lipstick won't hide neglected teeth. When you speak or smile your teeth become a focal point and they may spoil an otherwise beautifully groomed appearance or be the "extra plus" that makes you truly attractive.

### ROUGE HAS A DUAL ROLE

*Rouge is a color artist,* a feature builder. Colorwise, you should select just one shade. Rouge should be discreetly applied and correctly blended, and made to appear as part of your own natural coloring. It cannot, therefore, take on various hues that blend with your costume, but must always blend with your skin tone. In selecting your personal rouge, it's best to take a medium shade with the barest touch of pink in it, to make you look soft and pretty.

*Rouge and the forehead.* For a low forehead, apply rouge somewhat lower than ordinarily; for a too-high forehead, apply closer to the eyes.

*Rouge and the eyes.* For eyes too close, apply rouge from point under center of eyes, and blend toward and almost into the ears. For wide-apart eyes, start rouging at point directly under inner corner of eye, and blend off evenly at height of cheekbone.

*A very short chin* can be brought to pretty size by round, "invisible" rouging. A square chin can be rounded by rouging the center with a well-blended dot; a pointed chin, by rouging its sides.

*To avoid obviously rouged cheeks,* put one dot on the widest part of your rouge areas, grin or smile, and blend the color up and out according to the natural smiling contour. Under no circumstances should you apply rouge in a circle.

*Don't apply makeup too heavily,* even if you have to apply two kinds of foundation, plus rouge, plus powder. "Make down" with the minimum amount of each, spreading evenly, blending perfectly.

*Avoid mask contour.* Although you can't see the area between the edges of your cheeks and your ears when you face the mirror, your critics can. So, don't stop short. Continue your makeup right to your ears, pull it down even to your ear lobes, and see the natural glow your whole makeup takes on.

*Makeup applied under an electric light* may show up quite differently by daylight. Try to apply your makeup in light as close as possible to that in which you expect to be seen.

### CHOOSE YOUR FAVORITE MODEL

*Pick her carefully.* Many women, especially the younger set of beauty seekers, secretly select some current beauty of the stage, screen, or TV after whom to pattern their beauty scheme. Too often, however, they select an inappropriate model for their own particular kind of beauty, and the results are unnatural and far from lovely.

*Find your double.* Remember that there are different kinds of blondes, brunettes, brownettes, and redheads, so be sure to find the one who resembles you in many ways. For instance, there are the small, fiery redheads like Susan Hayward; there are redheads with goddess-like proportions like Rita Hayworth; there are queenly redheads like Greer Garson.

*Never forget that you are you.* Use these lovely women of the stage and screen as models from whom to get ideas for your makeup, your coiffure, your fashions, etc., only because they are groomed by experts in the grooming arts, and not because you wish to look and act exactly like them. Then, adapt the ideas you gather so that they may enhance your own individual personality and make you a more beautiful, well-groomed "you."

*If you'd be a lucky bride,* here are some important suggestions that can help you to look your most beautiful on your wedding day. The most important thing to remember is to look your own, natural self. Never try to look like someone you have seen in pictures or at another wedding. If you are a glamour type, be a glamorous bride. Don't try to be a fragile beauty. If your beauty is of the fragile type, remain true to this beauty and don't try to be a glamour girl.

*Plan the coiffure* you'd like to wear several weeks in advance and learn how to handle it properly. Many girls make the mistake of having their hair set into a brand-new style the day before the wedding, and because it is unfamiliar, their nervous fingers don't know how to handle the curls and waves, and the result is anything but beautiful. Often, the style you are wearing is the best, and will look the most beautiful when you don your veil.

*Your makeup should appear natural.* Apply all of the beauty requisites that you usually apply for your own special occasions. Select them in shades that harmonize with your complexion. Your wedding day is no time to play with new tan or rosy foundation makeup shades, exaggerated eyebrows, or lip patterns. Likewise, the girl who is accustomed to applying many beauty requisites should not walk down the aisle looking like a ghost.

*Apply all your makeup* before you put on your wedding gown. Nervous fingers often drop anything they hold, and a lipstick falling down over your spotless white dress would spell disaster. Allow yourself enough time for your makeup and hair, so that when your bridesmaids adjust your gown and veil, when you hear the music that will float you down the aisle, you'll be one of the most beautiful brides of the year.

## ALL THROUGH THE DAY

*To start the day,* and to go on quick, use an all-in-one makeup. That's a creamy powder from a pressed cake in a skin-matching shade. It goes on like powder, has the cling and the covering qualities of cream. Puffed on a clean face from hairline to neckline, it will make your skin look as velvety as a Georgia peach from early in the morn until long past Pop's first big yawn at night.

*In the morning,* wear pale lipstick. That's enough color for 8:00 a.m.

*When it's time to reach for a late-day lipstick,* a blazing red to brighten your face and lift your spirits, it's time for touch-ups. Unlike loose powder that can look spotty if confined to one area, touch-ups from a creamy-cake makeup can be localized. To banish the pallor of fatigue, puff on a bit of dry cake rouge at the end of the day. Brush all powdery traces from eyebrows, and give them a once-over-lightly with a sharp eyebrow pencil.

*Eyelash makeup goes on quicker,* looks smoother, stays put longer (even while slicing onions), if you'll use hot instead of cold water to work up a paste.

### TEEN-AGE MAKEUP TIPS

*The barest minimum of makeup* a youngster needs depends a great deal upon her personal coloring. To create a better color balance between skin and hair, this is the reason why anyone, young or old, wears makeup in the first place.

*The vibrant brunette* with fair skin will need only lipstick to complete her color contrast.

*The girl whose hair,* eyelashes, brows, and skin shades are almost the same tone will need more lipstick to break up the uniformity of color. She should be allowed (note to Mother) to wear a discreet touch of cheek rouge.

*The youngster who is to wear a foundation* should be given a compressed cake-type. This is the perfect blend of makeup base and powder and takes no skill to apply. No matter how inexpert she is, she can't use too much, layer it on, or look obviously made up while wearing it.

*Makeup for young diploma takers* or young girls otherwise under glaring lights: Nervousness and the auditorium's lighting can conspire wickedly against the girl graduate while all the world is wishing her well. Suppose she goes as pale as her white dress when she steps up on the stage? The remedy for that is prevention, a blush-pink makeup.

*Makeup to make a young girl look delectable* is hardly more than a tinted powder. What more there is, however, is a creamy base to make powder cling, to kill the shine on a soap-scrubbed face; if need be, to hide any adolescent blemishes. With this makeup, a pink or coral lipstick shade looks completely correct.

*If you're a teen-ager,* accent your youth for all it's worth with the freshest appeal you can muster. If you're wearing a dark lipstick, give it away. Beg, wheedle, or baby-sit for a party-pink lipstick, as delectable as pink-ribbon lacings in a grownup baby dress.

*See that the fresh pink lipstick* goes on as clean a face as you can bring up from the basin. If you need to kill a soap shine, puff on powder from a cream cake, that is gentle to young skin. If there are adolescent blemishes to shush, the palest pink shade will help you keep your secret.

### TO HAVE AND TO HOLD THAT YOUTHFUL NECKLINE

*There are two major causes* of the unwanted, old-looking feminine neck that is ravaged with wrinkles, sags, double chins, and blotches. These two causes are "time" and "neglect." We can do little about "time," but so much can be done about "neglect" that the clock seems to stand still, and a lovely neck is the result.

*Lift your chin off your chest,* unfold your neck, and look up for beauty's sake. When you read, walk, write, think, drive your car, or talk, lift up your chin, hold up your head, and unfold the creases of your neck. By doing this you'll not only augment the beauty of your neck, but you'll also add grace to everything you do.

*Cleanse your neck* with cleansing cream every time you cleanse your face, and with the same enthusiasm. Also, be sure to continue the cleansing by washing your neck with soap and water, and rinsing it well, just as you do your face. Stimulate by applying skin freshener or astringent. Use skin freshener for dry skin and astringent for oily skin.

*Each night, massage your neck* for about three or four minutes with the same rich cream you use for your face. Massage with an upward stroke, moving your hands from the base of your neck up to your ears, your jaws, and your chin. Blot off excess cream and retire.

### HANDS ARE GOSSIPS

*Whether tapering and thin,* plump and dimpled, tanned and trigger-quick, gifted or lazy, hands have one trait in common: They're gossips that will shout out their tales of neglect. And they'll all protest cold weather with ruffled-up skin.

*To get the most from your hand lotion,* first soak hands in warm water to open skin pores. Massage as you work in the lotion. This manipulation will limber up hands that are never very supple in cold weather.

*Gloves were made to be worn,* not to carry. Wear gloves, even if the supermarket is only around the corner.

*Chapped hands crying for help?* Salvage a pair of worn, old cotton gloves, apply pure lanolin to your hands, slip on those old gloves, and wear them while you sleep.

*If you use strong detergents,* when you battle with pots and pans, wear rubber gloves into the fray.

*For longer, more attractive nails,* make a habit of pushing back cuticles with a towel after each washing.

*Brittle, cracked, or split fingernails* may often be due to overfrequent applications of nail polish and remover. When nails chip excessively, remove polish, treat with vaseline and hand lotion, but leave nail polish off for a few days, and watch the nails recover.

### FROM YOUR KNEES TO YOUR TOES

*Get on your knees* a regular diet of rich hand lotion, if knees are going to be exposed under Bermuda shorts or knee-high socks, in a bathing suit or tennis clothes. Rough knee skin can be rough on your over-all appearance. For comfort and for longer-lasting hose, follow hand-lotion routine on your soles and toes as well.

*Get rid of corns and calluses.* Both will go, if taken out of shoes with points of friction at toes and heels. To speed the departure of these blemishes, use corn pads on toes until the kernel can be uprooted. With a piece of pumice, work on the calluses every day after your bath.

*Give toenails even more care* than fingernails until they're out of the rough. Push back soaped-up cuticles while you're in the tub. File toenails straight across, but stop short of the toe tip. When you apply polish, align length of toes more perfectly by stopping the color short of the long toes, brushing color to the tips of the shorter ones.

*Down-at-the-heels on rouge.* Dare to carry rouge down to too-white heels. Even after feet are as tanned as nutmegs, the heels continue to stay an off-white. To subdue pallor, use cream rouge in a pink shade. A touch of pink rouge around pink-polished toenails is a sure-fire way of making

12-denier sandalfoot sheers give their money's worth of allure.

## CARRY YOURSELF LIKE A QUEEN

*To be serene,* and to "feel" well groomed is as important a beauty asset as physical good looks. Avoid clothes and cosmetics that make you do constant checking while you wear them.

*Wear a stole* that can be anchored, one that fastens with a self-fabric loop, buckle, or similar device.

*Keep the disheveling wind* out of your coiffure by either wearing a tie-on veil or spraying on a coat of lacquer that can be brushed out when you get to your destination.

*Wear a colorfast lipstick.* You won't have to fumble in your handbag, act furtively, or reapply too often.

*If you wear a strapless gown,* use double-face adhesive strip to keep it from slipping. Tugging up a gown can become almost as unattractive a public habit as pulling down your girdle or foundation garment.

*Sew tiny inside holders* to shoulder-line of garments so there's not a constant struggle with straps or bras and slips.

*Good posture hides waistline bulges.* When working, cleaning, or walking, remember to stretch to your full height, and keep your shoulders back, tummy in, rear under. Cultivate the good-posture habit and you'll soon be walking in beauty, go much longer before you tire.

*You're the fairy godmother who can do it.* Avoid pressure on any one spot of Baby's skull, by simply turning your baby from side to side carefully. It's almost entirely in your hands whether she'll have a beautifully shaped head or one that the hair stylists will have to camouflage.

*Teeth are so important to her future good looks.* See that her first full crop of 20 baby teeth get a close review by a trusted dentist. If teeth buck or bolt out of line, put them into braces when the dentist says it is time for them.

*Watch out for any thumb-sucking habit.* Correcting any habit that threatens to push her teeth out of line is the ounce of prevention now, worth nine pounds of lipstick "cure" later on to try to revamp an ugly mouth.

*Training for beautiful posture,* that is the dynamic keystone to all future good looks, should begin the moment you start picking up your baby. Firmly supporting her back with one hand, changing often from right to left, the arm in which you hold her, are the earliest steps in posture training.

*Bowed legs,* are ofttimes due to cooping a baby up in a playpen or other confined area. If she pulls herself up to see what's going on outside, legs not ready for body weight are apt to bow in or out. The same risk is taken if she is encouraged to walk before she's ready to support her weight.

# SHORT CUTS AND WIFESAVERS
# IN HOUSECLEANING

### HOW TO KEEP YOUR HOME SPARKLING—WITH LESS
### WORK, LESS MONEY, AND FAR LESS TIME

*Housewives in a hurry* sometimes forget that the vacuum cleaner needs brief attention at frequent intervals. Take a moment every two weeks to put one drop of oil in oil caps or oil holes (to keep the motor in better working order), and also to empty the dust bag faithfully if it gets too full and the motor has to work against back pressure. Disposable bags make this an easy task.

*Reassignment for discarded wire hairbrush.* Use it to remove hair and dirt from brushes of vacuum cleaner and carpet sweeper, a quick job that keeps these household tools in better working order.

*Scrub brush won't slip* from your hand, and will be easier to use, if you fit a drawer knob into the wooden back.

*New mop out of old socks.* Instead of discarding worn socks, clamp them into the holder of your mop and you have a fine new dry mop.

*Sponge hint.* Keep household sponges fresh by soaking them in cold salt water from time to time. Boil them out once in a while too.

*When chamois stiffens up,* soak it in warm water to which a spoonful of olive oil has been added. Your chamois will emerge as soft and clean as when you bought it.

*Your neighbor will love you,* if you don't shake dust mop out of the window. Lay it on the floor, on a piece of paper, then run the vacuum-cleaner nozzle over the top. Takes up dirt easily, quickly.

*Save time and work while dusting.* Be sure to dust high objects first, so that any falling dust can be gathered later, without your having to dust some things twice.

*To keep dust from accumulating in corners,* shellac the baseboards in your room. Not only will this make sweeping easier, it will make cleaning the baseboards a relatively simple task of merely running a cloth over the surface from time to time.

### IS YOUR WINDOW A SHOW WINDOW?

*Window cleaning hint.* After washing a window, dry it on the inside with a sideways motion, on the outside with an up-and-down motion. Then if any streaks remain to be removed, you'll know instantly whether they are on the inside or on the outside of the window by the way the streaks run.

*Keep Jack Frost away.* On cold days rub alcohol or salt water on the outside of your windows, then polish them with newspaper. Keeps windows defrosted.

*Spotless ledges.* Window sills can be cleaned with practically no effort if you give them a coating of wax. The wax protects paint. Rain and dirt wipe off in a jiffy.

*Easy wall or window washing.* First tie a sponge to your wrist with a string. Saves getting down from a ladder when the sponge pops out of your hand, also speeds up your work by freeing the same hand for your chamois cloth.

*Homemade solution* for cleaning painted walls can be conjured up by combining two ounces of borax, one teaspoon of ammonia, and two quarts of water. You'll need no soap. Apply with a soft cloth.

*Make wallpaper washable.* Cover it first with sizing, then with a clear shellac. A damp cloth will clean it easily thereafter.

*Trick for the wall switch.* The space around light switches sees a lot of traffic and, therefore, may be smudged frequently. After the space is cleaned, a thin coat or two of fresh, white shellac will make the area around the switch easier to clean. An occasional quick dab with a damp cloth will then keep the space clean.

## SHORT CUTS TO CLEAN FLOORS

*Floor surfaces wear better,* if you wash them very thoroughly before applying wax or shellac.

*How to clean linoleum.* Never flood linoleum surface with water. Use only wax on linoleum, never shellac, varnish, or lacquer.

*Inlaid linoleum should be waxed,* since varnish would tend to crack where breaks occur between inlaid pattern segments. Liquid wax is preferable to paste-type, because it's easier to apply. Apply thin coat. Too much doesn't dry hard and simply becomes gummy.

*Rug cleaner.* Before you vacuum your rug, sprinkle it with a solvent cleaner, then work in with a stiff-bristle brush. The vacuum cleaner will dislodge the heavier, embedded dirt, will clean and strengthen the tufts, and brighten the colors of the rug.

## YOUR MODEL KITCHEN

*It's easy to clean kitchen-range porcelain.* Wait until it's cool, because porcelain enamel is glass fused on steel and is breakable if misused. Use mild soap and warm water. Avoid cleaning powders and harsh abrasives that may scratch enamel finish.

*Broiler pan cleans easier*, the sooner you wash it after using. Don't leave uncleaned pan in oven, for stains will bake on and become difficult to remove.

*Sinks smell better*. A handful of baking soda put in the sink overnight will clean and purify the unfragrant drain.

*Rust remover*. Dip rusted metalware in pure cider vinegar, then let it dry for a few days. Wipe away the remaining, loosened rust particles.

*Keep faucets shining bright*. Rub the brass or other metal with furniture polish after cleaning.

### FINISHING TOUCHES

*Got those ring-around-the-bathtub blues?* Add a few drops of kerosene to the suds, and watch those telltale markers disappear like magic.

*Air purifier*. Replace hospital smell of antiseptic cleansers with fresh, perfumed fragrance by pouring a little cologne into a saucer and lighting it. Heating the cologne first makes it burn better.

# THE ART OF CARING FOR HOUSE FURNISHINGS

### HOW TO GET MORE, BETTER, AND LONGER SERVICE FROM THE THINGS THAT MAKE A HOME

*Don't be afraid to use your good china.* Instead of saving china dinnerware for special occasions, use it often, every day if you like. Its strength makes frequent use practical. Like your good silver, it grows lovelier with use.

*Care of china is simple.* Because of its durability, it's simple to wash fine china. Use a mild dishwashing detergent, washing and rinsing with water as hot as your hands can stand. Avoid harsh detergents, gritty cleansers, and steel wool.

*Most china can go into the dishwasher,* except for china that is decorated with material that can't be subjected to water as hot as is delivered to a dishwasher.

*Cracked dishes.* If the cracks are not too deep, you can probably make them invisible by boiling the dish in sweet milk for about an hour, over low heat. This is often a wonderful way to keep intact pieces that are hard to replace.

*Life insurance for glassware.* A glassmaker confides this nice little secret for strengthening glassware and making it less fragile: Put it into a vessel filled with slightly salted water that you allow to come slowly to a boil. The slower the boiling, the hardier your glassware.

*Make jars and bottles smell fresh.* Pour a solution of dry mustard into them, letting them stand for several hours; or use a diluted chlorine solution, then rinse in hot water.

*If one glass sticks to another,* don't try to force them apart.

Fill the glass on top with cold water, then dip the outer one in hot. They'll come apart without strain or breakage.

*Washing delicate glassware.* Glassware often cracks if put into hot water bottom first. Even very hot water will usually not hurt the most delicate glassware if you slip it in sideways, or edgewise, slowly.

*Save that nicked glass.* When that hard-to-replace glass does get nicked, wrap a piece of "oo" emery paper around the handle of a spoon and rub it back and forth across the nick until you've smoothed it down.

*To clean glass vases* that have become stained, add some tea leaves to warm water and let it stand in the vase for several hours. Empty, then wash vase out with hot soapsuds, and rinse in clear hot water. Another idea: Soak in strong solution of hot vinegar, then wash in clear water. Either way, the sparkle returns like magic.

*Scratchless mirrors.* To protect the back of a mirror from scratches, cover it with a coat of clear shellac. Another reminder: The sun will cause mirrors to become cloudy. Hang them away from direct sunlight.

#### WHEN SILVER GETS A CLOUDY LINING

*How to clean silver.* Place silver in one gallon of hot water, using an aluminum pan. Add one tablespoonful of ordinary salt and one teaspoon of soda. Then rinse and dry.

*Removing egg stains from silverware.* Knives, forks, and spoons, discolored by egg stains, are easily cleaned by rubbing them with salt before washing, then rinsing in soapy water, followed by a clear-water rinse, and drying.

*Rub furniture polish* on silver vases and frames, and notice how long it keeps them gleaming new and free of tarnish.

*Tarnishproof silver storage.* Wrap pieces of silver individually in tissue paper, and store in tall potato-chip can. Seal cover with cellulose tape, or store in airtight glass jars.

### OTHER HOUSEHOLD METALS

*Brassware needn't be hard to clean.* Instead of polishing frequently, clean once, then apply a thin coat of fresh white shellac. Second coat gives still more protection. After this treatment, brass keeps clean with whisk of dustcloth.

*Tarnished brass.* A lemon rind, dipped in salt, will remove most corrosion spots on brass.

*To keep pewter brilliant,* merely wash with hot suds, rinse, and dry. Silver polish will help.

*Copper beautifier.* Rub copper with salt and lemon juice or with salt and vinegar, and you'll have it clean and sparkling richly in a jiffy.

### AGE-PROOFING YOUR COOKING TOOLS

*"Season" your enamelware* by putting it in water and bringing it to a boil slowly. Lengthens its life.

*The cool treatment.* Always let metal cake pans cool before washing, to prevent warping of the metal.

*To "de-fish" or "de-onionize" utensils,* put a few drops of ammonia in the dishwater when washing used dishes. Or put several tablespoons of vinegar in the dishwater; fish and onion odors disappear just like that. Another quick deodorizer consists of washing, scalding, then inverting the utensils over a gas flame for about two minutes.

*Crusted casseroles.* When burned food is hard to clean from casseroles, fill them with warm water and add a teaspoonful of baking soda. The crusted matter will loosen quickly.

*Clean like magic.* A little vinegar and salt boiled in an iron skillet will remove its untidy black spots or burns.

*Iron pots and kettles* won't rust if, after washing, you wipe them thoroughly dry, and then apply a little lard or other grease.

### YOUR FURNITURE CARE

*When do you wax?* New pieces of furniture should be polished with wax or wax polish every two weeks. Later, once a month is enough. Wax protects surface against water or liquor marks.

*Wax wise.* Polish furniture or floor surface with cloth wrapped around a small sandbag. This adds weight, results in smoother work.

*Overheated rooms* will injure your finest pieces of furniture, and ruin antiques. Don't store extra table leaves in cellar or other damp areas. Avoid placing furniture against hot radiator or under open window.

*Give mahogany furniture a vinegar rinse.* Restore dull or blurred finish to its original luster this way: Wring out a soft cloth in a solution of vinegar and warm water. Wipe the surface of the furniture with it, and leave it on for a day or two. Then apply furniture cream or polish.

*Paper stuck to table surface* can damage finish, unless you take this precaution: Put a few drops of oil on the paper scrap. Let it soak through for several minutes, then rub gently with a soft cloth. Paper is then easily removed, without damaging finish.

*Furniture scratches disappear.* A little iodine, applied to a scratch on dark furniture, will nearly always erase the blemish or make it much less noticeable.

*Ideal care for leather furniture.* When leather shows signs of soiling, wash with a thick lather of castile or saddle soap.

Remove soap with damp cloth, then wipe dry. Occasionally use leather dressing to keep it pliable and prevent scratching.

*White rings vanish.* Unsightly white rings on highly polished furniture (from heat, etc.) will disappear upon applying warm, camphorated oil. Rub the furniture until it is dry, then polish with a clean, soft cloth.

*Happy dreams.* We hope you don't toss and turn at night, but if you do, squeaking bed springs won't bring on restful slumber. Instead of oiling the spring and thereby staining sheets, spray on liquid wax and out go the squeaks.

#### A NEAT PACKAGE

*What's in it?* Label each package before you put things away in your attic, basement, or extra closet. This will save you needless unwrapping, bewilderment, and time when you finally do want to locate some of the contents.

*To tie tight, secure packages,* use wet string. It shrinks as it dries and thus gets tighter.

*Waterproofed shipping labels.* To protect an ink-written address from being smeared by rain, rub over it lightly with a candle. The thin wax coating protects the handwriting.

*For safety and ease of handling,* pack books on end and one row deep in strong cartons or boxes. If box is wide enough for two rows, pack with books back-to-back. Saves the bindings.

#### TIPS ON THIS AND THAT

*Newspapers have many uses,* even after the family has finished reading them. Save for packing clothes out of season, or rolling in rugs put up for the summer. Newsprint also discourages moths. A well-crumpled newspaper is also handy for wiping windows dry, leaves no linty coating.

*Newspaper rug pad.* If you haven't a regular rug pad, use newspapers under your large rugs. Spread several layers flat under the rugs and you'll save wear, make the rugs look and feel better underfoot, make the floor warmer, provide a soft, luxurious tread.

*Shelf paper* won't tear so quickly if you secure it with scotch tape instead of thumbtacks.

*Ash tray gum.* Denatured alcohol does a miracle job of cleaning those black and gummy stains on ash trays.

*Removing cork from inside bottle.* A cork that has been lodged inside a bottle or decanter can be removed in this way: Pour enough ammonia into the empty bottle to make the cork float, then put the bottle away for a few days. By then the ammonia will have chewed down the cork to size where it can be poured out of the bottle.

*Smoke disperser.* Soak a towel in water, swish it around the room and watch how quickly smoke disappears. Another idea: Dispel smoke and other odors by leaving a saucer of vinegar in the room.

*Outwit the lid.* Those frustrating struggles with a jar lid that won't come loose can be eliminated by lining your hand with sandpaper before turning. You'll be able to grip like mad.

*For wet umbrellas.* A large sponge placed in the bottom of your umbrella stand will absorb the dripping water.

*Ants will hate you.* If ants are invading your household, it will help you to know that they are allergic to cucumber skin. Keep bits of it where ants congregate and they'll scram.

*When washing your lamp shades,* prevent the colors from running by turning an electric fan on the shades as soon as you've rinsed them.

*Leather book covers* need care, especially if not in constant use. When dusting, use a slightly oiled cloth occasionally, to restore some of the oil that has dried out of the leather.

*Books stay new-looking,* if you clean soiled top edges, spread covers apart, grip the pages lightly, and rub gently with fine steel wool or sponge eraser.

*Handles on the mattress.* If there are no loop handles on your mattresses, sew on some sturdy strips of ticking. They're very helpful when it's time to turn mattresses.

# CARE, REPAIR AND CLEANING OF
## HOUSEHOLD APPLIANCES AND GADGETS

### ELECTRIC POWER SPLIT THREE WAYS

*Branch circuits* are the small wires through which electricity is distributed to the outlets in your home. These branch circuits serve the same function that pipes do in carrying water through your plumbing system; the electrical outlets, where you plug in your appliances, correspond to water faucets.

*Your home's wiring system* should contain three kinds of branch circuits:

1. *General-purpose.* These circuits serve light fixtures all over the house (except the kitchen, laundry, and dining areas) and convenience outlets for lamps, radios, TV sets, phonographs, vacuum cleaners, and the like in every part of the house (except kitchen, etc.).

2. *Small-appliance.* These circuits bring electricity to the kitchen, laundry, and dining area convenience outlets that serve your refrigerator, toaster, mixer, coffee maker, and other plug-in relatively small appliances. On one of these branch circuits you can connect, at one time, a total of 2,400 watts. How many of this type of circuit you need depends upon the total number of watts required by the appliances you now have and those you plan to add later. Most homes should have at least two of these small-appli-

ance circuits. A large home may require three or more of them.

*Note:* Kitchen, laundry, and dining area lights require a circuit of their own. This separate circuit may, in addition, serve lights in other areas of your home.

3. *Individual branch circuits.* These circuits must supply power for many of your large appliances. Each piece of electrical equipment listed here requires an individual circuit of its own:

1. Automatic heating plant (for all types of fuel).
2. Electric range (a double-oven range needs a larger individual branch circuit than does a single-oven range).
3. Electric water heater.
4. Automatic washer.
5. Combination washer-dryer.
6. Electric clothes dryer.
7. Summer cooling fan (attic fan).
8. Home freezer.
9. Air conditioning unit.
10. Built-in space heater.
11. Electric workshop and workbench equipment.

*Look ahead when wiring.* Consider the appliances you have now and those you plan to buy in the future. Figure out from the outline above how many electrical outlets you will need in the future and where they'll be most convenient to use. Then call in an experienced electrical contractor and let him wire your home in such a way that electricity serves you conveniently, safely, and efficiently.

### MODERN APPLIANCES NEED LITTLE CARE

*Manufacturers are your friends.* When you buy household appliances, don't throw out the descriptive booklets provided by the manufacturers. They'll give you helpful hints on the "ounce of prevention" that will keep the appliance in shape for maximum time.

*They're longer-lasting than you think.* Many household appliances appear to have outlived their usefulness before they really have. If toaster, cleaner, washer, or other appliance gives you much trouble, don't immediately discard it for a new one. Instead, consult your dealer and see if replacement of some parts can make the appliance as good as new again.

*They run themselves these days.* All you have to do is turn on the switch and your appliance takes over your work for you. Because this automation requires intricate mechanism to operate, however, don't try for home repairs if something goes wrong. Manufacturers have skilled repairmen who will save you money and lengthen the life of your appliance if you call them in at the first sign of faulty operation. Just consult the classified section of your telephone directory to find the right repair service.

## YOUR REFRIGERATOR

*Modern refrigerators need no defrosting.* Defrosting is automatic these days. All you have to do to make the appliance give you full service is not to overcrowd the interior, clean it thoroughly every week or two, and give the exterior a regular application of a special wax finish designed for appliances with porcelain enamel finish. Use it whether yours is white or one of the new colored appliances.

*Quick defrosting.* If yours is an older model, try filling your ice-cube trays or pans with hot water. Repeat if necessary. The ice that coats the freezing unit will melt away in record time.

*Ice cubes in a hurry.* Store one or more large jars of water in your refrigerator. Use the water to refill ice trays. Since the water is already chilled, you'll have those extra ice cubes in jig-time when you want them for company.

*Jam-proof ice trays.* Ice-cube trays can be practically "stickproof" by rubbing oil or grease on the outside.

*Remove ice-cube trays* without a struggle by placing them on thin pads cut from rubber stair-tread material.

## CARE OF YOUR RANGE

*Your range should be level.* If floor unevenness makes your range tilt even slightly in any direction, you'll bake cakes that are uneven because oven shelves are not level.

*Don't let foods burn.* Wipe up food spills as fast as they

occur and you'll preserve the porcelain-enamel finish of your range.

*Set a pan of ammonia and water* in your range oven overnight. In the morning cleaning the oven will be a breeze.

*Commercial oven cleaners,* both solid and spray-type, do a quick job. Be sure to follow container directions for use, however, and be safe by wearing rubber or other moisture-proof gloves.

*Foil broiler-pan cleaning* with aluminum foil. Line the bottom part with foil to catch the drippings. Cover the top section with foil too, and cut slits in it where the top part of the broiler pan is slit to let juices escape to the bottom part.

*Following use instruction booklet* that comes with your appliance will give you longest possible service from the machine. Two common causes of washer breakdown are overloading and using too much soap or special detergent.

*You have a choice* of low-sudsing detergents now on the market and designed especially for automatic washers. Use amounts recommended on the package and in the booklet that came with your own washer, for best results. Don't guess; use measuring cup.

*Washer-dryer combinations* save space and save you effort of switching your launderables from one machine to another. Treat them as both a washer and a dryer in caring for them.

*Check your dryer lint trap* and empty it whenever there's some accumulation of lint. Failing to do this not only decreases the efficiency of the appliance but could also be a fire hazard.

*If any automatic appliance* becomes noisy, it's time to call a serviceman. In fact, you can often prevent trouble if you have an arrangement with your serviceman to check all your home appliances once a year.

*Your ironer roller* needs to have its cover laundered occasionally, the padding removed to give it a chance to breathe a little before you reassemble roller covering.

*The ironer shoe* may occasionally have a little starch stuck to it. You can remove it with a mild abrasive or fine steel wool but treat it gently.

*Allow your hand iron to cool* before putting it away. And then wind the cord around it neatly, to get longest life from the cord.

*Distilled water is best for steam irons.* If you run out of it and have the kind of refrigerator that requires defrosting, collect the defrosting water and use it in your steam iron.

*Sit down when you iron.* You'll find you can iron longer and with much less energy expended. If you prefer to iron standing, because you've done it this way for many years, do use an adjustable-height ironing board, and position it at the height that is most comfortable for you. Adjustable boards have a wide range of positions from sit-down level to a height comfortable for a tall gal.

*Like velvety-soft bath towels?* Who doesn't? Invest in one of the new laundry conditioning liquids that goes into the final rinse water when you launder. Follow container directions for the amount to use. And after the towels are dry, you'll be amazed at the difference.

### ELECTRIC HOUSEWARES

*To clean pop-up toaster,* never, never shake it or poke into it with a harsh brush. Better use a chicken feather to brush out the crumbs. There's usually a hinged tray at the bottom, however, that you can unfasten by placing the toaster on its side. Swing it away from the toaster on its hinge, and it's easy to clean.

*Here's how to clean your waffle iron:* Scrub the grids with a fine wire brush, then brush them with nonsalted oil. After this, heat the iron for about ten minutes to recondition it. Soak up excess oil with a piece of bread placed between the grids.

*A clean pot makes good coffee.* Run your automatic coffeemaker through a perking or other brewing cycle occasionally when you've put water and baking soda in the pot. Clean it thoroughly afterward with clear water, to be sure no trace of the taste of soda remains inside the pot.

*Fill it with cold water* between brewings if you use your automatic coffeemaker every day. Water absorbs unwanted odors and flavors that may develop in the appliance if stored dry.

*You'll have keen knives* if you keep an electric knife sharpener handy. A few strokes on each side of the knife and, pronto, it's sharp and safe to use again. Some sharpeners are even flexible enough so you can use them for scissors sharpening as well.

*Dutch ovens have gone automatic too.* They're colorful as well, and heat is controlled thermostatically.

*If your mixer gets noisy,* call a serviceman. Don't use any appliance that is in need of repair, even if it still works.

*Your gravy lumpy?* Put it in your blender and in seconds it will be smooth as can be. The blender's wonderful, too, for smoothing applesauce, puréeing vegetables, and many other things you'll find in the booklet that comes with it.

*You'll cook in cool comfort* if you have an air conditioner in your kitchen as well as a ventilating fan. Your appliance dealer will tell you the best location for each of these luxuries so they'll perform at peak perfection.

*TV's fun in the kitchen too,* even if you can't look at it all the time. The new little portables take up small space, can sit on a counter in the kitchen.

### YOUR SEWING MACHINE

*Modern versatile wizard,* or durable treadle, your sewing machine will give long service only if you keep it clean and well oiled. But use proper sewing-machine oil, designed for the purpose, and oil only as directed in the care booklet that comes with the machine. Too much oil not only does the machine no good but it comes off on the fabric when you sew.

*Stitch and tension adjustments* are very important for best operation of your sewing machine. If you have difficulty in making the adjustments properly yourself, call in a machine service expert.

*Follow the manufacturer's directions* about size of needle and thread to use when sewing with different fabrics. It's worth the seconds it takes to change needles for the improved sewing results, worth a trip to the store to buy the right thread for the same reason.

*Manufacturer sewing centers* and sewing sections in department stores have a wealth of information that's helpful to you in your home sewing work. They'll give you lessons, as well, at nominal charge, if you'd like to sew like a pro.

## YOUR VACUUM CLEANER

*Uprights are best for carpeting,* rug and cleaner manufacturers agree. Modern cleaners have disposable bags that make it easy to empty when bags are so full cleaner is no longer able to remove dust and dirt at top efficiency. Don't let the bag get too full, disposable or not. It's hard on you, your rugs, and your cleaner if your machine doesn't work to perfection because you have to go over the same area so often.

*Use those cleaner attachments.* They do a very thorough job for you and for many above-the-floor cleaning tasks, much better than you can do with dusters, cloths, and brushes.

*Clean the attachments,* especially the dusting brush. Wipe off all attachments regularly. Wash brushes in suds and water, rinse in clear water, and hang up to dry so bristles won't flatten.

*Having two cleaners is ideal,* especially in larger homes. Reserve your upright cleaner for rug and carpet cleaning. Use the other for smooth floor surfaces and above-the-floor cleaning.

## HOUSEWARES AND GADGETS

*Increase usefulness of old brushes* with lacquer. By applying lacquer at the base of a brush you keep bristles from shedding.

*Can openers need cleaning too.* The cutting wheel gets gummy with food in time and should be cleaned very thoroughly. There's one can opener that comes with a spare wheel so the one that needs to be cleaned can go right into the dishpan.

*How to firm a food chopper.* Place a piece of sandpaper under the clamp, with the rough side up, before tightening the screw to table or pull-out shelf.

*Egg beaters and potato mashers* wash easily and quickly

if you place them into cold water as soon as you've used them.

*Soak all cooking utensils,* if you haven't time to wash them up before dinner. They're much easier to wash later.

*Don't rush hand dishwashing.* If you use a good dishwashing detergent and plenty of hot water, you'll find dishwashing much easier if you let them soak in the water and detergent for a half hour before proceeding with the job.

*Kitchen tools need oiling?* Apply a little glycerin with eye dropper. If any accidentally gets into food, don't worry. It's harmless.

*Saucy sieve successes.* Sauce lumpy? Simply force it through a sieve, using a wooden spoon or rubber scraper to speed the process. Works as well with lumpy gravy.

*Solids won't go through your funnel?* Keep a knitting needle handy, the plastic kind that won't rust. It's perfect to use as a plunger in the narrow funnel opening.

# GAS-ELECTRICITY-PHONE BILL
# MONEY SAVERS

*Cool foods* before you put them in your gas or electric refrigerator. It takes more power to cool foods in the refrigerator than it does if you let them come to room temperature first.

*When off on vacation* or even a week end, save gas or electricity by turning the cold control of your refrigerator down to the lowest operating point, just short of the defrost position on older refrigerator models.

*Place your refrigerator* on a cool kitchen wall. If it's next to a range or other heat-using appliance, the cold-food-storage appliance works overtime.

*Your gas-range pilot light is* most efficient if you regulate the flame height until it is blue with just a trace of yellow at the top. And keep assembly clean. Newer gas ranges, with electric pilot ignition, use no gas at all when the range is not in use and provide a cool appliance as well.

*Cut-up potatoes,* that are to be mashed later, cook in half the time whole ones do, cutting your fuel bill in half. Saves you time too.

*Cut large potatoes* in half before baking them and lessen baking time. Simply rub the dried cut surface with shortening or bacon drippings, as you do the skin side of a well-pricked baking potato, and the resulting taste thrill will delight you while you save money by halving the fuel bill.

*Cook with retained heat* in either your gas- or electric-range oven that is so well insulated you have to open the door to let out the heat if a recipe calls for starting high and finishing low-temperature baking or roasting. You can turn the modern range oven off an easy half hour before end of cooking time and know your foods will be done to a turn.

*Let your oven cook whole meals* at once instead of a dish at a time. You'll save fuel costs, time and energy too.

*Turn down the heat,* after foods begin to cook on top of the range. You'll cut fuel costs and foods will neither burn dry nor be shaken up and made unattractive because of too-rapid boiling.

*If you're buying a new range,* ask about the new surface units that turn the heat down automatically after foods begin to cook. Initial range cost is a little higher than for those not equipped with these units, but you'll have years of economical and carefree cooking if you buy the latest convenience that does some of your work for you.

### YOU CAN SAVE ELECTRICALLY

*Cut down on light bulbs* by using one high-wattage one instead of several smaller bulbs. A 100-watt bulb gives 50 per cent more light than four 25-watt ones yet costs only a few pennies more per bulb than the small size.

*Don't skip the light bulbs* when you're dusting. Few homemakers realize that a few swipes with a cloth over a dusty light bulb can increase light by as much as 50 per cent. Be sure lamp shades are dusted on the inside as well as outside.

*Get in the habit* of turning off lights when you leave a room and do not plan to return to it for a while.

*Check your lamp shades.* Solid dark shades and dark shade linings reflect less light than light transparent ones. You'll see better with the light shades and room has a cozier look.

*Wall reflected light is free.* When you repaint, use white, or light pastel shades. Rooms so painted require far less artificial lighting than those with dark walls.

## TELEPHONE THRIFT

*Numbers are elusive.* Check the telephone directory before you dial. Wrong guesses, in most telephone booths, cost you a dime apiece. At home, overages may raise your phone bills.

*When you shop by phone,* write out your list first. This saves ordering time and call-backs on the things you're likely to forget without a checklist.

*Long-distance overtime* soon runs into money. Make yourself a conversation guide, before you dial by jotting down the main points you want to talk about. You'll be surprised at how many minutes this saves on a costly call.

*Nighttime call reminder.* Remember that night calls are lower-cost than day ones on long-distance phoning.

*Trick on long-distance calls.* Place an egg timer next to the phone. The hour-glass kind works on a three-minute schedule, will warn you when your lowest-cost three minutes are used up.

## HOW TO CUT HEATING COSTS

*Pull down the shades* at dusk and leave them down overnight. This saves fuel and gives you desired nighttime privacy as well. Fuel is saved because the shade partially insulates the window. (In the summertime, drawn shades help keep your home cool.)

*If your basement isn't heated,* you'll have cold floors and resulting cold feet in first-floor rooms. For maximum warmth, finish off basement with a full ceiling.

*Your car won't freeze at 40°F.* If your garage is heated, keep the temperature low to save fuel and because your car likes to be on the cool side.

*Your basement runs a temperature?* Check your furnace; if it's too hot, call a serviceman. Danger signals are browned warm-air ducts, and scorched floor joints over the heater.

*Install a heat regulator* for automatically controlled heat. It saves you steps and money at the same time you keep your home at a desired even temperature.

*Use your fireplace.* It not only makes a room cozy in winter but raises the temperature of the room by as much as ten per cent, especially if coal is burned in the fireplace. When fire is dead and fireplace has cooled, remember to close the damper tight as it should be when the fireplace is not in use.

*A piece of asbestos board*, placed over the fireplace opening, saves the heat, should you retire before a fire is completely burned out.

# BEAUTY HINTS FOR FLOOR COVERINGS

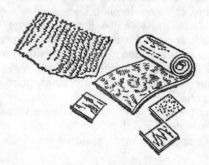

*Three "beauty hints" for floor coverings.* For long life, and beauty, practice the three rules of rug care recommended by the National Institute of Rug Cleaning:

1. *Clean daily* with a carpet sweeper or vacuum cleaner. The carpet sweeper is a handy tool and is especially good for frequent light pickups. Light vacuuming is equally recommendable.

2. *Carefully vacuum* your rugs once or twice a week.

3. *Have your rugs professionally cleaned* at least once a year.

*Turn your rugs around* to face in different directions once or twice a year. This helps to distribute the wear over their entire surface and adds extra years to their life.

*Clip the little tufts* or "sprouts" that protrude above the surface of your floor covering with a pair of shears, but don't —no, don't—pull them out!

*Lift furniture to move it.* If you push heavy pieces across the surface of a floor covering, you may damage the fibers seriously.

*Don't shake or snap small throw rugs* out of windows or doors when trying to dust them. The snapping action may break the yarns in the rug backing even though they are firmly bound. Instead, run your vacuum cleaner over them, with an upward motion at the end of each stroke to separate cleaner suction and rug ends.

*Let your professional rug cleaner* rebind worn edges of rugs and carpets. Amateur attempts to trim off such edges only result in greater unraveling.

*Cleanliness* is the best defense against moth damage. You can effectively discourage moth larvae from feeding on your rugs and carpets by daily vacuuming or sweeping and by using the professional rug cleaner's services at least once a year. If, for some reason, less frequent use of this professional service is necessary, apply one of the better-known moth-repellent sprays around the edges of the carpet and under all pieces of furniture three or four times a year. Food stains and other fatty or greasy substances should be removed as soon as seen. Under no circumstances roll up a rug and place it in attic, cellar, or storage room without first having it thoroughly cleaned.

*Take the "knives" out* of your rugs and carpets. Dirt is the accumulation of heavy soil particles and sooty deposits that either stick to the surface of the rug pile or work their way deep into it. Under constant footsteps, these sharp-edged particles cut rug fibers like hundreds of tiny knives, thus shortening its life. It cannot be vacuumed away. The grease in this dirt is often as high as ten per cent, causing particles to cling tenaciously to pile fibers. Your best defense against this enemy is the use of good professional cleaning at least once a year.

*Don't let shadows fool you.* Most rugs and carpets, as well as other pile fabrics, don't stand up straight. Instead, they have a natural slope in one direction known as the "lay" of the pile. You can help retard shading to some extent by always finishing off each session of vacuuming by running your cleaner with the pile lay.

# FLOWERS AND PLANTS

LIFE-PROLONGERS . . . ARRANGEMENT IDEAS . . .
TIPS ON CARE OF HOUSEHOLD PLANTS

*To revive drooping artificial flowers* quickly and effectively, hold them over the steam issuing from the spout of a fast-boiling kettle. Freshens the flowers right back to their original glory.

*Did you know* that flowers are good for fabrics? Cut flowers and growing plants not only bring life and color into your room, but the water you give them will add moisture to the air. This is healthy for you and your family, as well as for your furniture, draperies, carpets, and other textiles in the room.

*Ideal temperature* for keeping flowers is 40 to 50°F. High temperature and low humidity make for short-lived cut flowers. It's the low humidity that harms them when kept in the home refrigerator.

*Container must be scrupulously clean,* otherwise the soil, dirt, vegetable matter that accumulate, or are left over, will reduce the life span of fresh flowers.

*Stem ends of flowers* should never rest against the bottom of the container or the sides. Leave stems free so water can get to them and, through the stems, to the flowers. If you use proper holder, you can avoid not only this danger but the necessity of recutting stems every day.

*Always cut flowers with sharp tool,* whether with knife, garden shears, or scissors. Dull tools produce clogged stems that don't let water flow freely, and they harm the plant from which the flower is cut.

*Tools you need* to make effective flower arrangements efficiently: A small, sharp knife; needle-point holders; fine wire, sharp shears (for stems), waterproof clay (to anchor holders), shears (for wire), Parafilm (to tie stems), scissors, chicken wire (to put into containers and to anchor flowers).

*Cut off leaves below water level.* Leaves quickly decompose when submerged.

*Woody and semiwoody stems,* of lilacs, chrysanthemums, etc., live longer if the stem ends are scraped and split.

*Zinnias and marigolds* should be stripped of their foliage. These leaves are coarse and have a pungent odor. Substitute other greens with these flowers.

*Wilting flowers a headache?* Use aspirin to revive them. Cut flowers stay fresh longer than usual if you drop a couple of aspirins into the water.

*Basic designs of flower arrangements.* Consider the container, the style of the room, the spot in which arrangement is to stand. Then arrange flowers and plants by taking your cue from simple shapes like arcs, ovals, triangles, etc. Here are a few ideas to start you off:

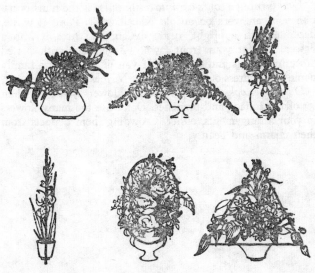

*Put your plants on an egg diet.* Save eggshells, put them in water, and let stand for several hours. Water plants with this liquid. The lime extracted from the eggshells will greatly benefit the plants.

*Tonic for ferns.* About once a week, water your house ferns with some leftover tea. Perks 'em up, helps them grow.

*Painted flowerpots.* Clay pots look dull. Make them gay and cheery by painting and decorating them to blend with the color scheme of your room.

*Two plants for one.* Break off the end of one of the stalks of a snake plant and bury the end about two inches deep in another pot. That's right. You'll have two plants for one.

*Fireplace garden.* An empty fireplace in the summer isn't very attractive. Fill up the space with a few potted plants, especially those with tall, heavy foliage.

*Like turning a sow's ear into a silk purse* is the transformation you can work on an old wheelbarrow. Paint it white, decorate with a bright, rustic design, and turn it into a flower cart for your front lawn. Fill interior with potted flowering plants and greenery. If you like, paint the family name and address on the side of the barrow facing the street.

*Don't overlook the proper foliage.* Flowers look best when set off by foliage and branches. Don't use too many flowers in your arrangements, either. Crowding them detracts from their charm and beauty.

# BE YOUR OWN DECORATOR

### WORK WONDERS IN YOUR HOME AT LITTLE COST
### . . . OR NONE

### CHOOSE WELL YOUR BASIC COLOR SCHEME

*Avoid vivid colors* for your basic color scheme. Softer, neutral shades are more restful and you are more certain not to tire of them. Reserve your bright color favorites for accent only.

*Color is the easiest tool of illusion:*

*Make a small room appear larger* by painting it a light, cool shade, either plain, or papered with an unobtrusive pattern.

*Make your large room look cozy* by applying a darker, warm shade to its walls.

*Pull down that high ceiling* with wallpaper bearing a definite horizontal repeat pattern.

*Lift a low ceiling* by painting it a pastel shade, and by putting vertical stripes on your walls.

*A north room,* with little sunlight, is cheered no end with a little light paint. Cover the walls with a pastel pinkish gray or a light yellow.

*A south room* receiving too much sunlight may need walls that absorb, rather than reflect, the glare. Here, darker shade is best.

*There are four basic color schemes* to choose from:

1. *Monochromatic* uses various shades of one color. The effect is subdued modern.

2. *Related motif* uses consecutive colors in the rainbow. For example: Groupings of green, blue-green, blue, blue-violet, and violet. The effect is modern and slightly more daring.

3. *Complementary* is usually complimentary as well. Don't use complementary colors, however, in equal strength. Decide which is to be your major color, and select a softer, lighter shade within its complementary color range.

4. *Split complementary.* Two complementary colors added to your major color. This is especially necessary in large rooms where your dominant color may be very bold by virtue of large wall space. A warm color must then be balanced by two cool colors, and vice versa. (*See "color wheels" below.*)

### MATCH FABRIC AND ROOM DECOR

*Fit the fabric to the style.* For modern rooms, select draperies and matching slip covers for a chair or two, or a sofa and chair, from the following materials: Chintz, organdy, mohair, linen, slipper satin, plastic fabrics, raw silks, novelty cottons, fiberglas fabric.

*Early American furniture* requires draperies of small-patterned chintz, calico, voile, or novelty cottons.

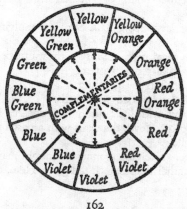

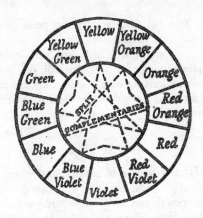

*Period style rooms* in Queen Anne, Chippendale, Hepplewhite, or Sheraton, look best with rich silk brocade, moire, damask, or chintz draperies.

### THE DRAPERY AND CURTAIN STORY

*Use pleater facing and hooks*, available at drapery fabric stores and such divisions of department stores, if you don't want to take the time to make the pleats the needle way.

*If you shirk shirring*, there's another drapery aid you can buy at your notions counter: A shirring tape that is quick and easy on the draw as well as on your time and energy.

*Don't align the lining.* Lining should be cut 3½ inches shorter and six inches narrower than the draperies themselves. Remove selvage from both drapery and lining fabric.

*Curtain rings in a jiffy.* Save time by getting poultry rings (in colors to match the materials in the room), and, without a single stitch, slipping them into the tops of lightweight or wash curtains. Takes only a minute to ring all the curtains in a room. You can also lacquer the brass curtain rods to match the room or curtains.

*Clip-on curtain rings.* There are very elegant curtain rings in brass and other metals that clip on, without stitching, that go wonderfully with curtain rods and other fittings. Most department stores will order them for you if they don't stock them regularly.

## YOUR SLIP COVERS

Even if fabric is washable, it's best to dry-clean slip covers and draperies. Why? In washing, they may get distorted and shrink just enough not to fit well afterward. Some of the heavier fabrics and trimmings, washable-dyed though they are, may contain excess dye that may bleed.

*If wash you will,* make sure the material, as well as the trimming, is indeed washable. Use only lukewarm water, and only fine mild soaps. If you cleanse in a washing machine, don't let it spin too long. If color runs while you are washing the article, rinse immediately several times in succession, until the last rinse water is absolutely clear. Hang to dry so that deep-colored parts can't drip on lighter sections.

*Put slip covers back on* while slightly damp. They'll smooth out as they dry, fit better than if you ironed them. Only the ruffles or pleats may need a bit of touching up. Even those, however, you can do after the slip cover is back on the furniture. Put a towel between the cover and furniture when you press the edges of freshly laundered slip covers.

*Hanging pictures?* Save the plaster. Before driving a nail into the wall when hanging pictures, stick a small piece of adhesive tape at the spot where the nail is to go, then drive through the tape. Helps prevent plaster from cracking.

*Thumbtacks prevent dust marks.* Place one thumbtack in each lower corner at the back of a picture frame, and the tack heads provide air space between picture and wall, prevent dust marks.

*Corking cutouts.* Cutouts in various designs, made from sheeting cork (the kind used for automobile gaskets will do) are attractive finishing touches for homemade masonite cabinets. Animal figures or characters from nursery rhymes are excellent in child's room; fruit, vegetables, and floral motifs will look attractive in your kitchen.

*Maps look important.* Here's an inexpensive decoration idea for your den or TV room: Put up a large pictorial map with colored pin markers to remind you of the places you have traveled to, or want to see. It's a smart idea that complements any library or television set.

*A clever partition* is achieved by hanging a Venetian blind from the ceiling. Ideal, for instance, when you have a large kitchen and want to partition off a dining area. The blind should be the same color as the walls, or should match the basic wallpaper color.

*Another Venetian-blind idea* works wonderfully when you want a good "door" to hang in front of a doorless closet or cupboard that you want to cut off from view while providing for ventilation.

## LAMP SHADES, LAMPS, LIGHTING

*Add a circular lamp shade* covered with same or matching material as slip covers. Circular lamp shades should be lined with fabric. For good stretch, both fabrics should be cut on the bias.

*To avoid rusting of lamp-shade frame.* Paint it with a primer, then with a coat of flat white paint. Allow to dry thoroughly.

*Match-dress lamp shades,* by adding tassels, moss fringe, or welting to match chairs near which they stand.

*Put your house in a new light.* If light outlets are poorly placed or insufficient, invest in inexpensive wiring job to assure adequate, more comfortable lighting. You'll cut down eyestrain for whole family and the rooms will look better.

*Unused light brackets* offer a wonderful decorative idea: Trim them with artificial hanging vines.

*Candles just for "show."* Candles used for decorative purposes only can be treated against drooping by giving them a coat of shellac. To clean, simply wipe with a damp cloth.

*More light, less current.* A single 100-watt bulb gives 50 per cent more light than four 25-watt bulbs.

*Add to the efficiency* of your lighting fixtures by having light-colored walls. You'll use less current for lighting.

*Emergency lamp when electric power fails.* Improvise by inserting string wick in a piece of cork. Float it in a glass filled with salad oil. Ignite the protruding end of wick.

*Best light from table lamp* is assured if the base is at least 12 inches high.

### LET'S EXPLORE THE ATTIC

*"Roll out the barrels."* At practically no cost, create a gay kitchen nook with old barrels as chairs, and gay fringe everywhere to add color and coordination.

*New furniture, practically free.* Many old pieces like kitchen chairs, will take on new life and beauty if all the finish that hides the natural wood is removed right down to the wood and then refinished so that the grain is visible. Those who have done this (and more are doing it all the time) feel that they have gained "new" furniture at practically no cost.

*Cut them down for new lease on life.* That old table or chest of drawers can be cut down and painted the same color as the walls of the room, to achieve a new, built-in look. Replace old metal drawer handles with solid flat brass pulls, yours at the five-and-ten.

*Find a kitchen cupboard in the attic.* An out-of-date chest of drawers makes a perfect base cabinet after legs are sawed off, to bring top surface down to work-table height. Then add shelves with plywood back and sides.

*Two files equal one desk,* like so: Set a plywood top across the surface of twin two-drawer files, separated by enough space for your legs to fit comfortably. Let your imagination and personal taste guide you in decorating it.

*Boudoir note.* Same idea can give you a serviceable dressing table, if you use two small chests instead of files, and add a pretty chintz skirt.

*Hanging bookshelves.* A clever, easy way to put in bookshelves is to cut them from fir plywood to the length and width desired. Then suspend them from the ceiling with black or white Venetian blind cord at the desired height. The weight of the books and other articles insures sufficient solidity and the cord makes a handsome line pattern against the wall. Closed plywood cupboard can be handled very effectively the same way.

*Make flowers grow on furniture.* Rescue some of the well-constructed, but worn-looking chairs, toy chests, etc., from dingy exile in the attic. Sand them down, add fresh coat of paint, then add floral or other designs that will make them different-looking.

*Attractive telephone directories.* Cover them with leftover swatches of wallpaper to match the decorative scheme of your room.

# MORE HEAT WITH LESS FUEL

### HOW TO CUT YOUR HOME HEATING COSTS FROM 8 TO 50 PER CENT—PLUGGING UP HEAT LEAKS— CARE OF EQUIPMENT, ETC.

*Unless you're a heating expert,* don't attempt repairs to heating units yourself. It's better economy to call in a qualified serviceman.

*"Preventive medicine" for heating units.* Just as you need an annual checkup by your doctor, so your furnace and boiler should be checked and cleaned once a year by a heating expert. Summertime is best. Have excess soot and scale removed; keep heating costs down. Additional summer treatment: Leave furnace doors ajar for free air circulation through firebox.

*So you've added a basement rumpus room?* Have you checked to make sure your heating unit is still adequate? Whenever you add a room or convert house space to new uses, check on this. You may be putting your present unit to extra strain, thus cutting its efficiency. Also, if you have cut off a room, you may need less heating.

*Don't burn garbage or trash in the furnace.* Doing so gives you a dirty furnace, clinkers, and poor heat. It also deposits a thick coating on the heating surfaces that absorbs the heat that ought to be warming your home.

*False economy.* Don't connect two heaters to the same chimney flue. This retards the draft and causes poor heat. If you have a separate gas water heater, a separate chimney will save you money.

*What comes out of the chimney?* If it's smoke, your heating plant is wasting fuel. Smoke is the result of improper combustion. Call burner serviceman immediately for checkup.

### YOU'RE NOBODY'S FOOL ON FUEL

*Those bargain-price fuels* are often of such cheap quality that they cost you more in the long run by giving less heat, causing lowered efficiency of heating unit, etc. It pays to buy fuel from a reputable, reliable source.

*The right fuel saves money.* A grade that's too heavy may cause excess smoke and soot; if too light, it will usually increase your fuel costs. Let a qualified heating man advise you.

*Cut fuel bills eight to 20 per cent.* Cracks and crevices around doors and windows cost you a lot in wasted heat. The best weatherstripping is a metal strip built right into the window sash or door. A less expensive type can easily be put on without special tools. The commonest and by far the cheapest type is felt stripping, about 10¢ a roll, and anyone can put it on.

*Why the fuel tank should be full,* even during summer months. It prevents the tank from "breathing and sweating" (caused by water condensation), accumulation of wasteful dirt and dust), avoids needless repair expenses. Exterior underground tanks left empty during heavy summer rain tend to "float" to the surface. Economy tip: Remember, fuel prices usually are lower in summer than during the heating season; another reason for filling tanks at that time.

*A pail a month.* To insure efficient operation of the hot-water tank, drain a pail of water from the bottom of the tank every month.

For *health and economy*, your thermostat should be set during the day between 70 and 72°F., normal indoor temperature throughout the year. An overheated house saps your strength, wastes fuel and money.

*When to turn thermostat down:*

1. If windows are open for any length of time, while airing rooms during house cleaning.

2. When you go to bed.

3. If room in which thermostat is located is closed off for airing, in order to prevent rest of house from overheating.

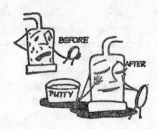

# DO-IT-YOURSELF HINTS

*You can plug a roof leak* from the inside quickly, in an emergency, by using roof cement on small holes, a rag and cement on those of medium size, and a board cut out to fit between the rafters for larger holes. Seal with roof cement.

*To raise wood shingles,* so you can repair or replace them, use a garden spade. The long, flat metal blade will let you get safely under the shingles. Press the handle down slowly.

*To replace a split shingle,* crack it up into slivers and pull them out. Cut the new shingle short, slip it into place, and nail.

*Don't paint asbestos shingles,* or you'll have to repaint every few years. A special cleanser, now available, will clean them like new.

*"Stitch in time" for tin roofs.* To avoid costly repairs resulting from extensive rust, keep surface covered with protective coat of special paint now being made for the purpose.

## WINDOWS AND SCREENS

*Windows sticky?* Paint the window slides with no-polishing floor wax or rub them down with the end of a candle. Tight windows are sometimes also caused by the divider moving out of place. To fix easily, rap the divider to one side.

*Petroleum jelly opens windows.* Once a year, take this precaution against hard-to-budge windows: Dip a small brush in vaseline and "paint" the ointment on casing and parting strips of windows. If windows have become stuck, pry open from outside, by inserting wedge or chisel under the sash. Before prying up, grease sash runners with vaseline.

*A cracked pane of glass* can be temporarily held together and weatherproofed with a coat of fresh, white shellac on the inside. Vision won't be obstructed by the shellac coat. Breezes and rain will be kept out until the pane is replaced.

*Small holes in window screens* can be patched by using a few drops of fast-drying model-airplane cement. Larger holes can be repaired by cutting a patch from a discarded screen and gluing it in place.

*Use a vacuum cleaner* on window screens to remove dust thoroughly and easily. If you haven't the new "snake-and-pot" type, turn your old machine on its back and run the screen over its mouth.

*The fastest way to paint* a screen is to use a rag or paint roller. First clean each screen thoroughly, then place it flat so that the paint won't run while drying.

### BE YOUR OWN PLUMBER

*To stop that faucet drip,* resurface the valve seat before you replace the washer. (This can be done with a handy tool that sells for less than a dollar at your hardware store.) Shut off the water. Take apart the faucet. Screw the tool into the faucet and turn a few times. (When replacing, be sure to use red washers for the hot water, black for the cold.)

*You can stop a drain-pipe leak* for years with a "plumber's poultice." Wrap layers of cloth and wet plaster around the leak. Use strong string to tie the "bandage" in place. Let dry before using.

*Quick rescue for frozen pipes.* Too much heat will make pipes burst because heat makes the ice inside the pipe expand. To thaw properly, fill bucket with very hot water and put heavy cloths in it. Wring out cloths and wrap around the pipes. As soon as cloths chill, reheat them and reapply.

*Only a drop in the bucket?* A faucet that leaks only one drop per second means a loss of 700 gallons of water a year. Check and repair immediately.

*Chipped porcelain-enamel sink or tub?* Cover it with a special enamel made for the purpose. It will still look somewhat patched but looks much better, in kitchen or bathroom, white than black or rusty. You can find sink enamel at your hardware store.

### WALLS, FLOORS, DOORS, WOODWORK

*To keep that crack from reopening* when you patch plaster, first scrape the crack clean, then wet it thoroughly before you plaster. When dry, coat the patch with shellac.

*Use two putty knives* instead of one when you patch with plaster. By using one wide and one narrow knife, you can keep both clean and much easier to work with.

*Slow that plaster down* so that you don't have to race against its inclination to harden fast. How? Simply add a little sugar or vinegar when mixing.

*Silence those floor squeaks* by dusting talcum powder or dripping glue into the cracks. (Works like magic.) Shellac the floor when dry.

*Remove floor scratches* by rubbing with fine steel wool dipped in floor wax.

*Remove rubber heel marks* by wiping the spots with kerosene, turpentine, or floor oil.

*Before you invest* in power-sanding your old floor, try washing it down with special, high-power floor soap. Use rubber gloves. In many cases the soap will restore the lightness and brightness of your dark floor.

*Quick trim for damaged woodwork.* It's not necessary to replace trim that has been damaged along the edges. Most times you can plane a new edge, and repaint. Even though the repaired trim may be narrower than its neighbor, and of different edge shape, the difference will be scarcely noticeable.

*Walls with moldings are dated.* The quickest way to modernize them is simply to remove the molding.

*Doors won't latch* as easily as they should when there is an accumulation of paint or dirt in the door-frame corner, when the bolt is sticky and won't extend easily, or when the latch has been pushed back out of place.

*Doors drag?* Try tightening the screws that hold the hinges in place. If they just won't tighten, fill the screw holes with plastic wood and try again when dry.

*So you're going to do it* the easy way. Hang a door? Slip some pieces of wood of the correct thickness under your door when you stand it up to locate the hinge cutouts.

*Creaky stairs* are nearly always caused by loose treads. If you can conveniently get underneath the steps, tighten the guilty wedges. If you can't, drive long finishing nails at an angle into the risers, through the treads. (Through the vertical sections, of course.)

*No need to remove the window trim* when you have to replace a sash-weight rope. Simply open the little trap door in the side of the slide. Loosen the screw you see there. Now use the old rope or a length of wire through which to feed the new rope. (Use sash chain for minimum trouble.)

### MINOR MENDS AND REPAIRS ABOUT THE HOUSE

*Homemade corks.* Satisfactory substitute for a lost cork is an inch or two of candle. Soften up the wax a bit and your candle "cork" is sure to fit. Or, if a cork's on hand but it's too large for the bottle, cut a small v in the side and, presto; it fits.

*For shrunken bottle corks.* Thermos bottle corks become compressed and too small from repeated use. Bring them back to normal by boiling them in a covered pan. Sterilizes them too.

*To remove dents* from pots, pans, trays, place dented surface against firm, level object (upturned flatiron often works), with bump surface facing you. Using medium-heavy hammer, tap the protruding dent with slow, light raps (heavy hammer blows will mark up the surface around the dent). A dozen blows or so will turn the trick.

*King-size ash tray* for your workshop. Use an empty coffee tin. Make lip for cigarette or cigar by snipping two two-inch slits down from the top and bending out the cut section. Double over the sharp edges. Water or sand in bottom of tin will extinguish the smoke and weight the "tray."

*Discarded auto license plates* make fine back-step scrapers. Your kitchen floor remains cleaner if muddy shoe soles are scraped out of doors. Nail old license plate to a corner of back doorstep.

*Mend breaks* in tooth-paste tube (or any other kind of tube) with a strip of sturdy scotch tape wrapped around the tube. Saves you money, keeps tube neat.


### THE LOWER LEVEL

*Damp cellar walls* can be dehydrated by painting with one or two coats of special cellar waterproofing paint.

*To smooth rough cellar walls,* try this mix: Two parts mortar cement to one part sand containing some calcium chloride. Add water to get a thin mud consistency. This produces a waterproof cement and may be applied before the waterproofing paint, with a large metal mason's trowel.

*Don't drill a hole* in your cellar floor until you consider the possibility that you may let in a stream of water. This is especially likely in damp areas where the cellar has been waterproofed carefully from the outside.

*Are plants piping water into your cellar?* Look carefully around the area outside your home. Dig up roots of trees or vines that may have penetrated the foundation walls, thus carrying moisture to them.

# HOW TO BE A HOUSEHOLD GENIUS

MISCELLANEOUS HINTS AND TIPS TO GUIDE YOU
TOWARD STAR BILLING IN YOUR OWN HOME

*Soften up hardened glue* by placing a few drops of vinegar in the container.

*Remove broken light bulb safely.* Press a large cork into the base of the bulb and unscrew it easily without having to touch the jagged edges of the bulb.

*Cold-wave solutions.* Usually stains from these do not show up immediately upon contact. It may take days, weeks, before they do. So, when having a home permanent, protect clothing completely. Not even your dry cleaner can guarantee stain removal results.

*Suede glove freshener.* Put gloves on and rub hand with thick slice of stale bread, changing to another slice as bread becomes soiled.

*Collect the dust.* Dampen the inside of the dustpan or broom bristles, before sweeping. This will prevent dust from flying.

*Extracting key if broken.* If you break off a key in a lock, run an old jigsaw blade into the cylinder alongside the broken piece and twist it so the teeth bite into the key. Pulling on the blade while in this position usually will remove the broken piece.

*A Christmas use for old lipsticks.* First melt down wax from old candles, shave the lipstick ends into the melted wax, and while it is warm, dip inexpensive white candles into it. They'll be beautiful and burn long.

*Extra protection for record albums.* Tape the cardboard liners that are used in wrapping them to the inside cover of the album. Leave bottom end loose so that you can lift the cardboard and read the program notes printed on the cover.

*When you open a new box of stationery,* paste a small envelope inside the cover. Use it to hold stamps and air-mail stickers, and you'll have them handy as needed.

*Don't waste shoe polish.* To get the polish that clings to sides of tin after center part has been used, hold tin over low heat. The wax will melt and form new cake of polish.

*A candle to the rescue.* When addressing packages in ink for mailing, protect addresses from smearing and becoming illegible, by rubbing a white candle over the writing. The wax coating forms a weatherproof protective surface.

*If you're short on eggs* or merely feel economical, substitute dissolved gelatin in croquettes or patty recipes that call for an egg to hold them together.

*Keeping track of the toddler in your home.* A tiny bell on the shoelace between the two bottom eyelets of the tot's shoe will save Mother many steps. You can hear where he is by the tinkling of the bell as he walks. Also, the child will enjoy the sound as he moves about.

*Junior won't lose his galoshes* at school if you try this: Give him a spring-type clothespin with his name on it. When he takes off his rubbers or overshoes, he can clip them together with the clothespin. He'll have no trouble after that.

*Junior's shoelaces have raveled tips?* He may have lost the tips during a hectic play period. Dip the tips into glue and allow to dry. Simple job saves you price of new laces, keeps old ones looking neat.

## A MISCELLANEOUS TOKEN OF TIMELY TIPS

*Inks and what to buy.* Permanent inks are for documents meant to last a long time and withstand possible exposure to water or strong light; if spilled, chances are it can't be removed without fabric injury.

*Washable ink* is for general use. If spilled on colorfast material, soak up as much as possible with blotter. (See stain-removal chapter for specific instructions.)

*Ink stains on fingers.* To remove them, moisten the stain, then rub with the sulphur end of a match and wipe with a dry cloth.

*Keep phone easy to reach.* Have telephone connected in spot that saves the most steps. If house has two floors, place phone on stair landing, rather than remote room on either floor, if you can't afford the luxury of an extension phone.

*A fair deal with cards.* If playing cards stick together, rub some talcum powder over them and you'll have a smooth new deal.

*When adhesive on envelope flap doesn't stick,* try quick application of nail polish. Dries quickly, leaves no smudge. Can't even be steamed open!

*Novel key ring at very low cost,* especially valuable to people who have to remove keys from ring frequently, is a simple metal shower-curtain hook.

*Paper clip* does double duty as a pencil clip. Straighten out one end and wrap it around pencil.

*Tired feet mean a tired you.* Two handfuls of ordinary salt in a basin of hot water give you new feet for old. Epsom salts, bicarbonate of soda, or ordinary brown laundry soap, make a mighty refreshing foot bath too.

# PAINT LIKE A "PRO"

*Keep mixing your paint thoroughly.* You must keep "boxing" your paint even though the machine at the store has mixed it for you. To do this properly, start with a container as large as the paint can. Pour half the paint into it. Mix both cans. Pour back and forth. Keep on mixing. Then take off just about the amount you expect to use. Remix the remaining paint at least twice a day, until it is all used up.

*To keep paint from crawling* off your kitchen wall, be sure to wash the wall down carefully with special cleaner and see that wall is thoroughly dry before you apply the paint. Remember, paint won't "stay put" on a greasy surface.

*Paint like a "pro."* Prepare for the job by moving everything into the center of the room before you begin painting.

*Single greatest cause of spatter* is the beginner's tendency to flip the brush at the end of the stroke. Others are the habit of dipping the brush too deeply, and the failure to clean the brush by pressing the paint out of the brush heel frequently.

*A cheap brush or an undersized one* tends to cause the painter to try to carry too much paint in his brush, the excess dripping off exactly where you don't want it.

*Lingering paint odors are passé.* Kill odor as you paint by adding a special chemical now available at your paint shop.

*Keep roller clean* and the paint well mixed (especially the water paints that settle very rapidly).

*Don't roll too fast* or you'll spatter.

*Don't dip roller* too deeply or paint will drip off.

*Use a large size,* generously felted or furred roller. An undersized roller is as bad as a poor-quality paintbrush.

*For getting into tight spots,* use a small brush.

*Rubber-base paints* need special handling because they tend to dry very rapidly. If you miss a spot the first time, better go over it hours later or you may pick up a section of half-dry paint. You may wash your brush or roller with water but, in most cases, rubber-base paints require their own special thinners and these do not use water. Also, rubber-base paints need a rough surface to bond properly. They'll always creep on oily, greasy, or enamel surfaces.

*Hold your brush short,* don't wear gloves, and paint first with one hand, then with the other, to avoid premature fatigue. Gloves do keep your hands clean but they tend to keep slipping, thus wasting your energy on merely gripping the brush as you try to paint.

### HINTS ABOUT EXTERIOR PAINT AND PAINTING

*How many coats of paint* does your new home really need? At least three coats of good paint for every bare-wood surface exposed to the weather. It's the third coat that adds years of good grooming to your nice, new home.

*Don't overdo it.* Enough is just right. In fact, many older homes suffer from too much paint. Such buildings are repainted when all they need is washing down. There's a special chemical, that you add to water, for this purpose.

*Good paint is good* for about four years on exteriors. Exposed paint wears down only about $\frac{1}{1000}$ of an inch per year. If the paint isn't permitted to thin, or if your house is repainted too frequently, the paint layer becomes so thick it will peel and crack off with no assist from you.

*When stalling pays off.* Never paint when the temperature is below 50°F., or when it is raining, when the wood is wet. The results will be unsatisfactory if you do.

*To paint border designs* like an artist, simply rent or buy border stencils and dab the paint over the openings.

*Mix putty and paint* to make a color-matching hole filler. Clever, huh? Works fine too.

*Skip a step.* When painting steps, paint every other one, then let them dry. Later paint the remaining ones. In this way the dry steps may be walked on without injuring the paint.

*Useful use for burned-out fuses.* When spraying paint, screw an old fuse into each socket within the area to be sprayed. Keeps sockets clean.

*Insects add nothing to a paint job.* Keep them from settling on painted surfaces that are still wet. Add citronella, cedar, or pine oil to final coat of paint. Teaspoonful or two to full pail of paint is enough, and won't injure the consistency of the paint.

*Large paper plate,* glued to bottom of paint can, catches all drippings and provides convenient resting place for brush.

*Toy bucket works for Daddy.* When Dad has a paint job to do, and the paint can has no handles, he can borrow Junior's sand pail, set the paint can inside, and presto, he's ready to go.

*Paint daub identifies color in can.* Save yourself time and wasted effort when hunting among your stored paints for the color you want. Apply a daub of the color at the level of the remaining paint in the can. That way, you can also tell whether you have enough for the job you want to do.

*Convenient, disposable paint containers* can be made from empty milk cartons. Cut container in half, rinse, and dry. Wonderful for holding small amounts of paint or varnish.

Straight side of carton is fine wiping edge for the paintbrush.

*Paint won't slop over* sides of the can when you replace lid if you take this precaution: Before using paint, tuck a piece of heavy twine in the lid groove of the can. Remove this just before replacing lid and there won't be any paint in the groove to drip over.

*Lost the cover of that leftover paint?* Here's a trick borrowed from the kitchen. Melt paraffin and pour it over the surface of the paint (the way you do over jellies and preserves). Paint will remain soft until needed again.

*Banish paint odors.* In a freshly painted room, place a large open pan of cold water containing a large onion cut in half. This time the onion goes to work for you. Paint odors will sponge up within a few hours.

### BEFORES FOR BETTER AFTERS

*Before you paint walls,* a first coat of fresh shellac will form a nice even base for the paint. The shellac will also prevent uneven absorption. Because shellac dries very quickly, the paint coat should go on the same day.

*Painted surfaces won't peel* precoated with shellac or aluminum paint before you paint. Be sure to remove all old and defective paint before applying undercoat.

*Before painting doors and windows,* smear locks with vaseline, so surplus paint will be easy to remove.

*Before applying enamel to brass,* prepare metal surface carefully. Wash thoroughly with any household cleaner that doesn't contain soap, then wipe down with denatured alcohol. Otherwise, paint won't stick.

### PAINTING AND DRYING TRICKS

*Make linoleum look new again.* Faded, worn linoleum can be made to look brand-new with an easy paint job. Ask your dealer for a special paint suited to the purpose, choosing a color to match the basic color of the linoleum. Wax when dry.

*Dust specks won't cling* to newly varnished furniture if it is suspended upside down to dry.

*When painting small pieces* of furniture, turn them upside down and paint the underneath portion first. Much more convenient.

*Painting flowerpots is easy* if you rest them upside down on suitable-size tin can. Can permits rotating pot without touching it, and provides good support to hold pot while it dries.

## THE CLEANUP

*Paint spattered on tiles* may be removed with a cloth dipped in turpentine.

*Paint-spattered floors.* Even when paint spatters have hardened on your floor, they are fairly easy to remove if moistened with nail-polish remover, allowed to soak in for a few minutes, then rubbed off with a cloth and washed with warm suds. They usually disappear no matter how long the spots have been there.

*Paint ain't.* To remove paint spilled on concrete floors or driveways, scrub with a strong solution of lye water, then rinse the floor well with clean water.

# HOW TO BE YOUR OWN HANDY MAN

SIMPLE REPAIRS AROUND THE HOUSE, AND OTHER
HOME IMPROVEMENTS, THAT BEAT THE HIGH COST
OF OUTSIDE HELP

*Hardware storage tip.* Store bolts, screws, washers, etc., in compartments of ice-cub tray. Compartments are deep enough to prevent mixing of contents.

*An antirust trick.* Keep few cones of carpenter's blue chalk in toolbox to absorb moisture. Every two months, dry chalk thoroughly in an oven to renew its effectiveness.

*Make your flashlight see around corners.* Clamp bicycle mirror to flashlight. Directs beam of light at angle and reflects articles at which it is directed. A clever convenience when doing repair work on car or on plumbing installations.

*Prevent after-mess in gluing jobs.* Place a piece of waxed paper on top of glued article before putting on weights, to help hold pieces together as glue hardens. Prevents weight from clinging to glued object.

*"Combing" in the glue.* To apply a thin coat of glue uniformly over a large surface, use a fine-tooth comb as a spreader. Especially handy when working on large pieces of veneer.

### ABOUT THE HOUSE

*If driving rain seeps in* under your outside doors, you can stop the leakage by making a shallow saw cut in the lower edge of the door where it stands on the sill. When the water gets to this little crack, it has a tendency to run back out of doors instead of coming on in. The saw cut, of course, must be on the outside edge of the door.

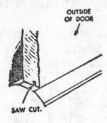

OUTSIDE OF DOOR

SAW CUT.

*Use a small syringe* to suck out chips and dust when cleaning out a blind hole or crevice.

*Run your drill* through the bottom of a cheese or ice-cream carton to catch the chips.

*To seal linoleum seams,* run a strip of cellophane tape down the full length of the crack. Shellac over the tape and the surface will hold up indefinitely. The shellac coat will not only prevent dirt from seeping through but will also prevent tripping.

*See your electric push buttons in the dark.* Simply coat them with a layer of luminous paint and you'll never have to grope to find a switch.

*Improvise a neat holder for small tools.* Small files, pliers, screwdrivers, etc., can be held in place and carried around conveniently while you work if you rack them into the closely packed bristles of a scrubbing brush. The inverted brush back makes an excellent stand to keep them upright.

*Make your own shoe rack.* Nail a metal curtain rod on the back of the closet door. Hang shoes by their heels over this rod. If necessary, use the whole back of the closet door, nailing several rods one below the other, and allowing sufficient space between the rows so that shoes won't touch.

*Make your own rubber bands.* When you discover holes in your rubber gloves, convert them into rubber bands instead of throwing them out. With a pair of scissors cut across the width of each finger, the palm, and the wrist. You'll have quite a few first-class rubber bands of different sizes, cut just the thickness you want.

*Two chests for one.* Chests that are too high can be sawed in half and made into two small ones that fit into spare corners.

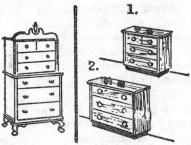

*Use for an old radio*, now that TV is here to stay. Remove the "innards" of the old console radio cabinet, add shelves, slick it up with fresh paint, and presto, a bookcase or writing desk stands before you.

*Protect an outdoor padlock*, by nailing a rectangle of stiff leather on the door above the padlock. This little "roof" over the lock keeps ice or snow from dripping into the lock where mechanism might rust or freeze in cold weather.

*To clean a file*, place a strip of adhesive tape lengthwise over it. Rub finger over tape, to press it firmly between file teeth. Then pull it off. Imbedded shavings, dust, etc., come off easily with tape.

### HOME GROUNDS

*Plant a "children's row" of flowers* in your garden. Youngsters can pick their own bouquets for teacher, you, or for a friend. They'll enjoy the pride of something all their own, and very likely won't go snipping any of your favorite blooms.

*Safe perch for a birdhouse.* Birdhouses can be fastened to the top of a pole in your yard, with the help of a large tin can. Screw the house to the underside of the can, slip the can on top of the pole, and nail it in place.

*Rack keeps gardening tools handy.* Tack strips of leather to sides of wheelbarrow to form loops. Loops are excellent holders for various tools.

*Reduce erosion damages* to your lawn and grounds by setting a large flat stone under your rain spout. This will spread the rain water over a larger area and help to prevent the wearing away of your precious topsoil.

*Don't ruin your tires* by running them over a hole in your asphalt driveway. It's easy to patch the holes with a bagful of stone and tar mix. Leave the bag in the sun or near a warm radiator to soften it up, and be sure the cavity to be filled is clean and dry. Tamp your patch firm with the end of a two by four.

*Wire coat hangers* take to the out-of-doors. When you want to direct a light spray of water on shrubs, flower beds, etc., and you have nothing on which to support the hose nozzle, bend a wire coat hanger into shape as a stand and use the hook to hold the hose in place.

*Birds don't like blue.* Birds won't eat your grass seed if you color it with bluing before spreading it. Soak seeds in solution of bluing and water until well colored, then scatter. Birds won't touch them and coloring doesn't affect fertility of seed.

# BIG IDEAS FOR SMALL FRY

### EASY-TO-MAKE CONVENIENCES TO MAKE THINGS EASY FOR YOUR CHILD

*Safety-first diapering.* Stick pins into a cake of soap kept handy on the table or bed where diapers are changed. Makes pin points easier to pierce diapers with, avoiding pinholes in sheets and mattresses. Also keeps pins out of Baby's reach.

*Ouchless pins.* A decorative pot holder attached to the wall several feet above the crib or dressing table provides a safe, handy place to park open safety pins while changing a baby's diaper.

*Rainbow bath.* To make the bath a real treat for the kiddies, add a few drops of vegetable coloring to the bubble suds. The resulting scads of gaily colored bubbles that float about will delight your child.

*Handy storage for Baby's buoy toys.* Use net bags from potatoes, onions, or oranges. Hang out of the way on clothes-line or bathroom hook. Toys will air-dry quickly and be handy for the next dunking.

*What does Baby weigh?* If you have a bathroom scale, but not one for baby weighing, you still can determine infant poundage. Step on the scale with Baby in your arms, then get off and put Baby down. Now step on the scale again. The difference is what Baby weighs, of course.

*Protect Baby in the rain.* If it's raining when you take Baby out in the carriage, rainproof him by covering the blankets with a plastic tablecloth.

*Gift wrapping for the kiddies.* Add gala touches by thrusting a few lollipops into the knot of the bow, or by wrapping package in comic paper instead of regular gift wrap. Another idea: Attach a dime-store trinket to your wrapping ribbons.

*For your little girl's birthday cake,* try using tiny kewpie or baby dolls instead of candles. They're inexpensive and mean an extra gift of a dolly for each of your child's little guests.

*Do Baby's pull toys slip through his fingers?* He won't lose them half as often if you make a soft handle for him out of an old rubber jar ring. Attach string of the toy to the ring, and Baby is all set to navigate further.

*Save wear and tear on children's games.* Shellac the board of such games as checkers, parchesi, etc. Keeps pasteboard in better condition; it can even be wiped off when soiled by play-begrimed little hands.

*Interesting use for old broom handle.* Use a handsaw to cut circular disks and save them to replace checker pieces which children so frequently lose. After disks are sanded smooth, paint them to match the missing checkers.

*Bunk partitions.* Two bunks, one above the other in children's room can often serve as a partition forming a partially private room for each youngster. Do it this way: Fasten a piece of ¼-inch fir plywood on one side of the lower bunk so that it closes off one side between the lower and upper. On the other side, close off the space between the upper bunk and the ceiling. The result will be two room areas, one for each youngster.

*A gift from your hardware man.* Ask him for empty nail kegs. Painted and decorated, with the addition of a cover, they can serve as children's hampers, stools, or as scrap baskets, and containers for kindling wood.

*Roll-away toy boxes.* Here's a simple way to eliminate under-bed toy clutter. Get Hubby to put together two or three sturdy plywood boxes, then mount them on casters. Keep the height low enough so that the toy containers can be rolled under the bed when not in use.

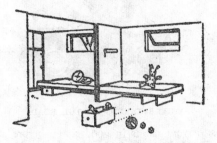

*For that student in your family,* a helpful memory aid. A small bulletin board made of builder's wallboard and simply framed, then placed above his desk, is a good place to tack advance assignments or other study memoranda. And a wonderful way to communicate for the kid who loves to exchange notes.

# THE FAMILY BUGGY

TO KEEP DOWN THE UPKEEP ON YOUR CAR, JUST
TRY THIS HANDY CHECKLIST OF MONEY-SAVERS

YOU'RE TAKING TO THE ROAD?

*Make sure your car* is in good shape before starting off on a trip. For a short trip (a few hundred miles) get an oil change and a lubrication job and have the tires, battery, and radiator checked. For an extended trip, have the above done and also have the following checked: Brakes, steering wheel, lights, horn, windshield wipers, mirrors, exhaust system, ignition system, wiring, fuel system.

*Hats always in the way?* Fasten stout cord across the back of the car's front seat. To it attach spring-type clothespins, as many as you have hats to hang up when not worn. Clothespins hold hats securely in position in this compact storage spot.

*Watch the temperature gauge.* Fuel burns at 4000°F. If the cooling system isn't working properly, this extreme heat can do a lot of damage to your pistons, cylinder walls, and other engine parts. The best operating temperature is between 170°F. and 190°F.

*Flush the radiator twice a year,* when removing antifreeze in the spring, and when adding it in the fall.

*Check the fan belt.* If too loose, tighten it; if frayed, replace it. A belt that doesn't work right can waste gasoline, cause cylinders to score, and leave you with an undercharged battery.

*Trouble's abrewing* if you look under the hood and see worn or frayed wiring. Have something done about this at once by your garage mechanic.

*Lacquer protects car wiring.* Apply coat or two of clear lacquer to exposed wiring in your car, particularly near the engine. Prevents acids and moisture from damaging insulation, prolongs life of the wiring.

*Look at your heater hose too.* It may be rubbing at some point. Keep hosing as well as wiring as far from hot engine parts as possible.

*Check your brakes,* if car tends to pull to the left or right. Check both front brakes, not just the one on the side toward which the car pulls.

*If your automatic drive acts up,* take your car to a mechanic at once. Correcting the failure is a job for factory-trained experts.

*Lubricate every 1000 miles.* Spending a little here can save a lot in terms of added power, better gasoline mileage, longer bearing life, and many other less tangible results.

*Keep the gas tank filled* so there's no room for condensation to form and cause grief by watering the fuel.

*Excessive oil consumption* can sometimes be traced to an overzealous gas-station attendant who fills the crankcase above the recommended level. Always keep the oil between the "add oil" and "full" marks, not above and not below.

*Never race a cold engine.* It burns a fearful amount of gasoline and, incidentally, greatly increases motor wear.

*Use your choke sparingly,* if your car is equipped with one. Since too much choking can consume up to four times as much gas as the engine needs, never leave the choke knob out further or longer than is necessary to get the engine running evenly.

*During first ten minutes engine runs,* operate slowly, shifting from low to second at ten miles per hour, from second to high at 25 miles per hour. If you have automatic drive, let the motor run for a while before you take off.

*At all times* start, drive, and stop smoothly. Fast acceleration at any time wastes gas. So does pumping on the accelerator when waiting at a traffic light. And so, believe it or not, does hard braking because it means that you have used fuel needlessly to build up too high speed for the conditions under which you're driving.

*A weak spark plug* may prevent complete combustion of the fuel. To prevent this, have spark plugs, distributor points, battery ignition coil, wiring, and connections checked regularly.

*The carburetor can waste gas* by providing too rich a mixture. Hence have the carburetor and fuel pump adjusted either twice a year or every 5,000 miles and keep the air filter clean.

*Sticking valves,* those that are warped and do not seat properly or have excessive carbon deposits, cause "pinging" and loss of compression and thereby waste fuel. This is overcome by having the valves ground and the carbon removed.

*Worn piston rings* should be replaced because they also cause loss of compression and allow valuable gasoline to escape unburned.

### EASY DOES IT

*If you must drive* extra-long hours, avoid heavy foods and stimulants. Substitute instead light, energy-providing snacks made up of fruit juices, cookies, and chocolate bars. These will keep you going and at the same time won't cause drowsiness as heavy foods tend to do.

*Start early and stop early.* Since there's less traffic on the road during the early morning than during the afternoon and evening, make a habit of early starts. And since hotels and motels fill up quickly late in the afternoon, start looking for a likely place to sleep around three in the afternoon.

# INDEX